ARNOLD BENNETT

ARNOLD BENNETT

by

KENNETH YOUNG

Edited by Ian Scott-Kilvert

PUBLISHED FOR
THE BRITISH COUNCIL
BY LONGMAN GROUP LTD

LONGMAN GROUP LTD
Longman House, Burnt Mill, Harlow, Essex

*Associated companies, branches and
representatives throughout the world*

First published 1975
© Kenneth Young 1975

*Printed in Scotland by
Her Majesty's Stationery Office at HMSO Press, Edinburgh*

ISBN 0 582 01232 5

CONTENTS

¶ENOCH ARNOLD BENNETT was born on 27 May 1867 at Shelton near Hanley, Staffordshire. He died in London on 27 March 1931.

ARNOLD BENNETT

I. INTRODUCTION

IT IS not every writer who, forty years after his death,
is quoted in a company report at an Annual General
Meeting. However, in April 1974, it was thought that
the fictional AGM reported in Arnold Bennett's novel,
Imperial Palace (1930), was relevant to the situation of the
London Savoy Hotel Limited and so extracts were read to
shareholders. Bennett, despite his inexplicable denials, had
based his exhaustively detailed study of a hotel on his
observation of the Savoy, from the laundry to the kitchens,
the restaurant, the ballroom and the private suites. He loved
de luxe hotels, not least the Savoy whose menu still faithfully
offers *omelette Arnold Bennett* (main constituent: finnan
haddock).

Fame, indeed! But, forty years on, how goes his literary
reputation? He wrote almost compulsively, publishing
around eighty books of all kinds between the age of thirty
and sixty-two when he died; he told friends in 1931 that
'I love work . . . the only thing worth living for.' One
at least of his novels, *The Old Wives' Tale* (1908), is accepted
as a modern classic, studied at schools and universities. Not
far behind come the *Clayhanger* series and other fiction set
in the Staffordshire of his youth, more particularly in the six
(not, as he said, five) small towns where pottery and table-
ware had been manufactured for a century; thus the area
was known as the Potteries. If popularity is to be judged
by paperback reprints, then Bennett is still popular: half a
dozen of his novels and short story collections are available,
as is his excellent Journal (though abridged) which he kept
from 1896. In recent years, some of his stories have been
turned into plays, films and television serials. His letters are
published in three carefully edited volumes by the Oxford
University Press. The literary causeries he wrote for the
London *Evening Standard* have been reprinted in a well-
produced volume. Nor does biographical and critical interest
in him flag. A young novelist, Margaret Drabble, born

eight years after his death, published in 1974, a personal, moving tribute to the man and his work; and one of the best biographies of any English writer is Reginald Pound's *Arnold Bennett* (1952).

Critics who do not care for his work always existed. Certainly he is highly criticizable, in the main because his output is as uneven as a crazy pavement and some of his themes are unworthy of his gifts; to other themes his inspiration would not soar. This, however, was not the real burden of complaint by such as Ezra Pound, Wyndham Lewis and Lytton Strachey, who sneered rather than criticized. His success, his yachts and his five shillings a word for articles in the press stuck in their maws; unlike some of his detractors he was a public figure, the cartoonists' joy, the darling of fashionable society. Worse still, his writing, though often subtle, was never obscure; so the young intelligentsia despised him. He was also a thoroughly dangerous pricker of inflated reputations; his writing in A. R. Orage's influential Edwardian periodical, *The New Age*, tumbled idols and tore up reputations, as one of his biographers puts it, and between 1926 and 1931 in his weekly column in the London *Evening Standard*, he was in Hugh Walpole's words 'the only man in my literary lifetime who could really make the fortune of a new book in a night'—or, of course, not. For long, critics, with the shining exception of the Frenchman Georges Lafourcade, and Frank Swinnerton, blamed him for not being Virginia Woolf, a line she herself took in *Mr Bennett and Mrs Brown* (1924); or they suggested that nothing he wrote was any good after he lost touch with his roots in the Potteries. The one was ludicrous, the other untrue.

He was 5 ft 10 ins in height, rather burly and, writes Swinnerton, 'One shoulder was always held stiffly, rather above the other, and he walked slowly and very erect.' He brushed his hair up into a quiff; below his moustache were rather prominent teeth. He affected startling bow-ties and wore fobs on his watch-chain. He had a life-long paralysing stammer. He was on terms of friendship with a very broad conspectus of his literary contemporaries—Wells, Conrad, Buchan, Galsworthy, Gide, Walpole, Maugham, Aldous

6

Huxley, Swinnerton. They liked him and he them. Wells wrote that Bennett 'radiated and evoked affection to an unusual degree'; and the generally prickly Maugham went further: 'It was impossible to know him without liking him.' He was a kindly man, generous with pecuniary help to such younger writers as D. H. Lawrence (who in return referred to him as 'a pig in clover'), and T. S. Eliot when he was starting the famous *Criterion* magazine; he gave his time and advice to such as J. C. Squire, Middleton Murry, the Sitwells, Noel Coward. He was almost everybody's literary uncle.

Yet in some ways he was a monster—the monster he looked when his face contorted into an almost animal snarl as a result of his stammer. His favourite sister, Tertia, wrote of his shattering silences, his 'terrible' moods when she was afraid to go near him or even utter a sound in his presence.

II. LIFE

In Bennett's life there was no high—nor even low—drama. It was a Jamesian or Trollopian life—though resembling in detail that of neither—rather than Wellsian or Dickensian. He was born at Shelton near Hanley, Staffordshire, on 27 May 1867, and came of a line of Methodists, such as those pictured in *Anna of the Five Towns* and *Clayhanger*, men and women cast in the Northern mould who, despite a concealed sentimentality, did not wear their hearts on their sleeves and kept the display of emotion for religious revivalist meetings, often very emotional indeed. His father, Enoch, had been a master potter, then a draper and pawnbroker; by dint of gruelling nocturnal study, after a long day's work (shops then were open at least twelve hours a day) he qualified as a solicitor at the age of thirty-four when Arnold was nine. Arnold's mother was daughter of a tailor in Burslem, one of the Pottery towns, though her grandfather had been a small farmer: by all accounts a pleasant, unassertive woman, dominated by her husband, to whom she bore nine children, three of them dying in infancy. The family situation, poor when Arnold the eldest was born, gradually improved and they moved to better accommodation. Bennett's father was an autocrat, not to say bully, who appears in fictionalized form in such of his son's novels as *Clayhanger*. Arnold went to two local schools, one of which had as headmaster Horace Byatt who was later to be H. G. Wells's headmaster at Midhurst. At Newcastle-under-Lyme Grammar School, Arnold passed the Cambridge University local examination, but his father wanted him as his clerk, so he never went to university.

When he was in his later teens he told his friend, Beardmore: 'I'm going to get out of this.' By 'this' he meant in part the dirt and provincialism of the Potteries. Passing through them by train many years later he wrote: 'The sight of this district gave me a shudder,' though in a letter as early as 23 December 1898, he noted 'a very real beauty underneath the squalor and ugliness of these industrial districts'. He also wanted to escape his father: 'I hated the thought of my youth,' he wrote, the fact being that he had never been allowed to be young. Escape, but how? One key to the door of his provincial prison was Pitman's shorthand, then rapidly being recognized as an important new office technique. In it he attained a speed of 130 words a minute. He was also writing gossipy notes for the local *Staffordshire Sentinel*. Above all he was reading—Ouida, George Moore, Zola, Balzac, de Maupassant, Flaubert, Turgenev, who remained prime influences on his fiction for the rest of his days.

He obtained a shorthand clerkship with a firm of lawyers in London. Thus he escaped and was never again to live in his native county. The pay was poor and his colleagues thought him 'too temperamental' for the law; often gloomy; not easy to get on with. But he found rooms with congenial people, some of whom remained lifelong friends. He began buying and selling second-hand books and in his landlord's house organized musical evenings. Bennett could play the piano; he could also sing (without a suggestion of a stammer). He practised his hitherto schoolboy French. He began to meet artists, architects, musicians and writers. One of them, G. K. Chesterton, remarked about Bennett at this time that he looked like someone who came up for the Cup and had failed to go back.

His first piece published in London was a parody for *Tit-Bits*; his second was a short story for the prestigious magazine, *The Yellow Book*, in which he appeared alongside Henry James, Gosse and Housman. Nothing could better symbolize his life-long capacity for succeeding in literary fields poles apart. He worked on his first novel, *A Man From the North*: 'the damnedest nerve-shattering experience as ever was.' When it came out in 1898, it evoked a letter of praise from Conrad but the profit from it, Bennett said, 'exceeded the cost of having it typewritten by the sum of one sovereign'.

He obtained the assistant editorship of *Woman*, partly because his father inexplicably bought shares. It was a paper appealing to intelligent female readers; under the pseudonym, 'Barbara', Bennett did a weekly column of reviews, and this was how he first met H. G. Wells, with whom he was an intimate for the rest of his life. As 'Marjorie' he did gossip and wrote 'Answers to Correspondents'. He said: 'I learnt a good deal about frocks, household management and especially the secret nature of women.' He learnt, too, the art of sub-editing. Proof-reading, however, was not his forte. It was he who, to the delight of Fleet Street, let through: 'Mr. Y., the rising young politician, made his first pubic speech . . .'

Soon he progressed to editor of *Woman*, a role he greatly enjoyed, not least in its social aspects. It is the only parallel between his career and Oscar Wilde's. He wrote reviews for the superior journal, *The Academy*—two worlds once more. And he played tennis, took up the craze of cycling, painted watercolours and was a good draughtsman. Always, wrote his friend the artist, Frederick Marriott, Bennett was 'to be found among the pioneers of any new movement'. In due course he studied calligraphy, of which his manuscript of *The Old Wives' Tale* is at once a model and a miracle. He found joy in classical music and art galleries.

Once again in 1902 his versatility was demonstrated; he published the finely achieved *Anna of the Five Towns* as well as *The Grand Babylon Hotel*, which would now be called a comedy thriller and was probably influenced by the highly popular works of E. Phillips Oppenheim, a contemporary who, however, began writing ten years earlier than Bennett; Oppenheim, too, achieved the status symbol of owning a yacht.[1] *The Grand Babylon Hotel*—the first of a number of hotels to be described in Bennett's fiction—was written as a serial; so were other sadly undistinguished books during the next few years: *Hugo, The Gates of Wrath, Teresa of Watling Street.*

But the success of these pot-boilers enabled him to fulfil an ambition: to live in Paris. He took a flat there in 1903 when he was thirty-five. France, of course, was the land of the writers he most admired; Paris, too, was the city of liberation where sexual matters undiscussable in England were discussed—as he put it, *sans gêne*—even between the sexes. To Bennett and some of his contemporaries, Paris had glamour, sophistication, *la vie de bohème*; to others it was the sink of vice. Both aspects are portrayed in *The Old Wives' Tale*. Gradually he made friends in the city, not only with writers and artists but with *demi-mondaines* vaguely connected with the theatre. He proposed to a young American girl and was turned down. He married a Frenchwoman, Marguerite Soulié in 1907; she had been connected with the theatre, though latterly and more successfully with a dress shop. It was in Paris that he conceived and largely wrote what is generally regarded as his masterpiece—*The Old Wives' Tale*. Of his years in Paris he wrote in his journal that he there enjoyed 'about as near regular happiness as I am ever likely to get'. Yet, as always, he suffered his neuralgias, his glooms and the desolate feeling of time passing. 'Today', he wrote on his birthday, 27 May 1904, 'I am thirty-seven. I have lived longer than I shall live.' His forecast was correct.

Bennett found no comfort or strength in the Christian

---

[1] Born a year earlier than Bennett, Oppenheim, who also came from the Midlands, published his first novel when he was twenty-one and became highly successful before Bennett set pen to paper. His output was even faster than Bennett's—thirteen full-length books, for example, between 1894 and 1898. Oppenheim bought his first country house while Bennett was still in a Paris flat and before long had a villa on the French Riviera. Like Bennett he worked in the Ministry of Information during the first World War. Like Bennett he had a taste for luxury. Unlike Bennett one of his lifelong luxuries was the seduction of women. Unlike Bennett he never wrote anything of lasting value, though he lived to be seventy-nine.

religion, and indeed had no time for it. 'Christian dogma sticks in my throat', he wrote in reference to G. K. Chesterton's Roman Catholicism. To Wells, in April 1905, he confided that 'religion is done for—any sort of religion.' However he studied and to some degree practised the stoicism learned from Marcus Aurelius and Epictetus; he was affected also by the theosophist Annie Besant's *Thought Power* (1901); he studied Christian Science. In later years he found solace in Eastern philosophy and in mystical passages in the New Testament which, he wrote in his 1929 journal, are 'perhaps the deepest source of private comfort'.

Some of these influences were not entirely beneficial since they buttressed an innate obsessional rigidity in his character, and that God-and-man-defying self-reliance which were the obverse of his kindliness and goodness. Epictetus and Annie Besant—strange coupling!—scarcely relaxed him. 'Habit of work', he wrote in his 1908 journal, 'is growing on me. I could get into the way of going to my desk as a man goes to whisky or rather to chloral.' By October of that year, 1908, he had already written 375,000 words. The pen was his favourite narcotic. He began to boast: 'My control over my brain steadily increases.' That emotional ebb and flow, which most human beings know, was to him the enemy of concentration, and was 'clumsy living'. He wrote books with such titles as *The Human Machine* (1908) and *Mental Efficiency* (1912). In the latter he thus sternly harangued his mind: 'You are nothing but a piece of machinery; and obey me you *shall*.'

His will, he thought, was all-powerful, but his flesh revolted. For his near-inhuman drive and determination he paid in sleeplessness, exhaustions, headaches and depressions. One doctor friend had long ago told him, in a phrase then common if imprecise, that 'You are one of the most highly-strung men I ever met.' Bennett wrote in 1912 that, while his income has risen to £16,000 per annum, it had been a year of 'intestinal failure and worldly success.' He suffered several bouts of gastro-enteritis, or possibly typhoid, long before the attack that killed him. He carried about with him a large collection of pills and nerve tonics. It should be added that he was rather greedy with food, though not with drink; the cocktail habit and 'leaning up against bars' he particularly abhorred.

The years in France (1903–1911) were productive. Apart from *The Old Wives' Tale* (1908)—which received immediate critical acclaim though it sold only slowly at first, he brought out a book of good short stories, *The Grim Smile of the Five Towns* (1907, containing his masterpiece in this genre, 'The Death of Simon Fuge'). He wrote the novel *Buried Alive* (1908), curious but excellent reading, the impressive *Clayhanger* (1910), some of it actually written during a stay in Brighton, and the ever-popular *The Card* (1911). He paid a highly profitable visit to the United States, returned to settle in England, bought a yacht, a car, and a country house at Thorpe-le-Soken in Essex. It is interesting that the larger part of his earnings just before the war came not from his novels but from his play, *Milestones*, first produced in March 1912; another play, *The Great Adventure*, a dramatized version of *Buried Alive*, also ran to 673 performances in London alone.

He was forty-seven when the war broke out in 1914. In many influential articles he accepted the Allies' aims, as did Wells, while firmly rejecting war as an instrument of policy. He spoke out for the 'squaddy', demanding that soldiers and their dependents should be adequately paid: 'To say that patriotism should be above money is mere impudence in the mouths of the elderly rich.' He toured the trenches and came under fire; he wrote patriotic and cheerful articles about the morale of those manning them. Yet his journal is strangely uncommunicative; he never made fictional use of what he saw at the Front, though there are references to wartime London. What he saw, this hypersensitive man, was very far from cheerful; but the recording of the gore and disgust he left to Sassoon and Graves, Remarque and Owen. During the war, he lived regularly in his London clubs to be nearer the centre of things and so saw the Zeppelin raids (one vividly described in *The Pretty Lady*). He sat on local and national committees with many persons well known in London society. It was not until May 1918, that through his friend Lord Beaverbrook—each found the other irresistible—he was given the top administrative post (unpaid) in the Ministry of Information which Beaverbrook headed. Official records of what Bennett actually did are non-existent, though he worked an eight-hour day, five days a week. When the war ended he rejected a proffered knighthood, though he would have appreciated some recognition (CH, OM?) as a writer; approached again later to accept a knighthood, he retorted, 'Give it to Harry Lauder' (the Scottish comedian and singer); 'They' did. Official honours were the subject of Bennett's successful comedy play, *The Title* (1918).

A first-rate novel, *Lord Raingo* (1926) came in part out of Bennett's experiences in the Ministry, Beaverbrook providing the Cabinet detail and without doubt some of the sketch of a character closely resembling Winston Churchill. Two more top-class novels came in the 1920s, *Riceyman Steps* (1923) and *Imperial Palace* in 1928; and at least two eminently readable novels, *Lilian* (1922) and *Accident* (1929). His journalism proliferated though his new plays fell flat. He became chairman of a committee which made the Lyric theatre, Hammersmith, one of the theatrical high-flyers of the inter-war period. He was a director of the left-wing periodical *New Statesman*.

Bennett took no direct part in politics. He had an inbred and stereotyped distrust of Toryism which, having been brought up a Methodist, he equated with the Church of England and did not understand. Though he had an anti-pathy to the Liberal leader, Lloyd George, he supported 'progressive' causes such as that of the suffragettes. He wrote forcibly in many a novel about the suppressed lower orders. From the cushions of his own much-enjoyed luxury he confessed: 'I am obsessed by the thought that all this com-fort, luxury, ostentation, snobbishness and correctness, is founded on a vast injustice to the artisan class.' Visualizing Midlands colliers boarding a tram he says: 'Set yourself to wonder why they don't use their brute force to wreck the tramcar. But they don't. They vote, many of them, Tory. Why?' However, unlike his friend Wells and the Fabians, he had no visions of utopias or benevolent dictatorships. Never in his plays or fiction did he, as did Galsworthy, starkly set the haves against the have-nots. Mildly, though probably accurately, he observed that 'the uncompromising democratic idea' was felt only by a few thousand men and they were far removed from those they would help, though, he thought, 'the abyss must narrow every year'. *Clayhanger* vividly presents what Bennett saw as the suffering, and fortitude, of industrial England; and *Imperial Palace* was perhaps intended to picture the idle rich living on top of slaving human beings—though the strengths of the book lie elsewhere.

Bennett's marriage to Marguerite ended in 1921 by separation, not divorce, and his financial settlement for her was very generous—too generous in view of his future commitments and his relative decline in earnings. A year or so later he began a new and happy life with the attractive and intelligent Dorothy Cheston—an actress—by whom he had his only child, a daughter. How then can it be said that this generous, hard-working man, upright and decent in his life, was a monster? Small matters first: he was a martyr to punctuality and martyrized those nearest and dearest to him who were unpunctual. He was neurotically obsessed by order, precision and regularity and was capable of going into aggressive sulks and silences if he thought the papers on his desk had been moved even by the fraction of an inch. He was extremely testy about the failings, real or imagined, of servants. His driving of himself to produce so many thousands of words a year was inhuman, yes, but not only to himself; his wife in particular suffered. It was in his relations with his wife Marguerite that his monstrosity becomes plainest. From the early months of his marriage he went off by himself—he was a travel addict —or with friends, leaving her alone. He did not take her with him on his first triumphant trip to the United States, nor on most of his subsequent peregrinations. She languished at home while he was on his yacht with his friends including females. At one time, though they were not on bad terms, they communicated by letter while living in the same house; they even had two separate flats in London. Doubtless Marguerite, a strikingly handsome and talented woman, had her faults and irritating foibles, but certainly during the early years of marriage she loved and cherished him and did her best to make him happy. Too often, however, he spurned the proffered marital bed and her company. It was not surprising that, during the war, Marguerite became interested in the young officers entertained at the Bennetts' country house, nor that she should have spent time abroad with a young Frenchman said to have been a neurasthenic war victim. Yet Bennett was far from being uninterested in women; he was no crypto-homosexual. He was in fact constantly pondering the inner nature of women, as his journals show, and he shows great insight into their ways; witnesses abound from Anna Tellwright, Hilda Lessways, Constance Baines to Gracie Savott. He undoubtedly had intimate relations with women before he married, perhaps with those anonymities mentioned in his journals, Chichi, Jeanne, Cosette, May Elliott. Yet he was the antithesis of promiscuous.

The Beardmores, to whom he was related, claimed in *Arnold Bennett in Love*, published in the franker days of 1972 and using newly available material, that 'He was dependent upon her [Marguerite] sexually, for constitutionally, out of inbuilt reserve, it is extremely doubtful whether he could have brought himself to undertake a chance liaison.' Of course, if their words were carefully chosen, they would not preclude a less evanescent relationship. They note, too, that he was titillated by black lingerie and what he refers to as *nouveautés nocturnes*. The Beardmores quote from letters between husband and wife shortly before their separation: Marguerite refers to Bennett's 'abnormal sexual habits' to which he ungallantly replied: 'What about *your* sexual habits? You didn't learn anything from me.' Bennett once expressed a desire to sleep with a negress but, as far as is known, did not. He may well have had sexual eccentricities, and in the novels there are hints of perversities. Most of his fiction, including *The Old Wives' Tale*, are drenched in implicit sexual atmosphere; later in *The Pretty Lady* and *Imperial Palace*, episodes become nearly but not quite explicit.

But in any case it was not promiscuity that proved the troublesome factor in his marriage. Bennett was simply not made for marital domesticity. His ideal way of living would perhaps have been that of G. J. Hoape—known like Bennett himself by his initials—in *The Pretty Lady* visiting regularly the respectable courtesan, Christine; or Raingo with Delphine in *Lord Raingo*. Socializing and party-going was one thing; having around him all the time a woman to whom he had duties and obligations was another. Whatever is the opposite of uxorious, he was. Even his latter happy years with Dorothy Cheston were punctuated by absences, not least when she, being an actress, was on tour; sometimes he grew impatient even with Dorothy, for as his admiring biographer, Margaret Drabble, admits 'he was not an easy man to live with'. It is an understatement.

In the 1920s Bennett was socially ever more in demand. Those with whom he dined or week-ended read like a list compiled from *Debrett* and *Who's Who*. Hostesses such as Lady Colefax and Ottoline Morrell competed for him, his friendship with Beaverbrook grew closer and with him he visited Berlin and Russia. Russia under the dictatorship of Communists, Bennett concluded, was 'an autocracy—that is a tyranny—far more complete than that of the Czars'. He was remarkably shrewd in a period when his friend Gide and the Webbs and many others of less integrity were so gullible.

Was Bennett a snob? No, but he was sought out by snobs. They wanted to hook him, not he them. He was famous, perhaps the most famous, certainly the most publicized, literary lion of his time. He enjoyed his fame and his fortune, perhaps even enjoyed seeing a drawing of himself on the sides of London omnibuses advertising his weekly review in the *Evening Standard*. But he made a nice response when the young novelist, Louis Golding, asked whether he was pleased to be recognized wherever he went. 'It *is* rather wonderful,' Bennett replied, 'in a disgusting sort of way.' To a few his flamboyant dressing seemed vulgar; even his friend Wells referred jocularly to his fobs as 'Arnold's gastric jewellery'. Others thought his retention of his Midlands accent a little ostentatious; and he did rather over-do his 'grand hotel', *train de luxe*, yachting image. Fame brought no cessation of his neuralgia and headaches. He was often depressed believing that his financial situation was not as secure as it once was. He gave up his yacht—'you can't have a baby and a yacht too,' he decided. Yet he went on giving to funds for 'starving geniuses', reading their works with enjoyment, even those of James Joyce, though confessing he could make nothing of Gertrude Stein.

In what proved to be the last few years of his life, Bennett began to behave out of character, not to say eccentrically. He who could not suffer noise and slept badly took, against Dorothy's advice, a flat over Baker Street station in London. Lunching at Hugh Walpole's apartment, he was angered that there was no sweet course, so angered that he left abruptly, took a taxi to the Ritz, had his sweet and returned to Walpole for coffee. He had, wrote Dorothy, become 'adamant and brittle' with a 'curious rigidity'. His death may be ascribed to defiant obstinacy. One night in Paris, he, so fastidiously careful about health dangers, drank from the tap water, ignoring Dorothy's reproaches. When shortly afterwards he did it again in a restaurant—despite the waiter's 'ce n'est pas sage, Monsieur', the least Freudian-minded might be forgiven for murmuring 'death wish'. On his return to London, typhoid was diagnosed and—with Marguerite hanging about in the vestibule and straw strewn outside to deaden the traffic noise—he died on 27 March 1931.

The headlines thundered his death; the obituarists were gracious, even Virginia Woolf, observing that his passing 'leaves me sadder than I should have thought', and Rebecca West summed it up: 'All London will miss him, and some Londoners will miss him very bitterly. For he abounded in kindliness.' Despite his forebodings he left £36,000, securities valued at £7,900, copyrights at £4,225; by 1975 standards, it was probably the equivalent of a quarter of a million pounds.

III. FICTION

For all his versatility in different genres of fiction, most of his novels and short stories bear trademarks recognizably Bennettian. There is the miser as early as *Anna of the Five Towns* (1902) and, twenty-one years later, in *Riceyman*

Steps. He frequently and at his best analyses, with curiosity rather than sympathy, the discord between the sexes, why men and women can simultaneously hate and love each other. His heroines are either 'comfy' like Alice Challice in *Buried Alive*, or wayward like Hilda Lessways; his *cocottes*, of whom he presents quite a few, are on the whole 'comfy'. Elderly women are either defeated or slyly bossy. His young men are shy and repressed, the middle-aged cautious yet dreaming romantic dreams, and indeed acting them out. Old men are overbearing and distrustful.

His serious novels are slow-moving in action, almost static: Debussy not Beethoven. This results from his calculated technique: the action of the novel must 'spring out of the characters and the characters should spring out of the general environment'. To this, events, plot are subordinate. Instead, in practice, Bennett concentrates on assembling details observed and chosen to create an impression of verisimilitude, the coherence of a character and background. He belongs in part to what Hardy calls the 'life in a plain slice' school. Hence for instance his minute description of the diseases—ranging from measles and angina to double pneumonia and cancer—which are to carry off his main characters. And Hardy's criticism is valid: 'A story must be worth the telling and a good deal of life is not worth any such thing.' At the same time Bennett is deeply concerned with presentation, form, technique. Yet his austere realism and the slow build-up very far from preclude strange twists to stories and surprises for readers; and in his best fiction, this evokes not incredulity but the reader's assent, 'Yes, that must have been exactly how it was.'

These qualities are little evident in his first not very good novel, *A Man from the North* (1898), about a young clerk from the Potteries failing to write a first novel, despairing and choosing the quiet, safe suburban life. The hero, as Margaret Drabble points out, is an Arnold Bennett who failed; the Arnold Bennett who wrote it did not. Psychological shock there certainly is in his second novel, *Anna of the Five Towns* (1902), where at the denouement the eponymous heroine realizes that she is in love not with the smooth, competent, kindly Mynors, but with Willie, the naïve, lanky, pathetic son of a recently-failed pottery maker who had committed suicide—'She had promised to marry Mynors and she married him. Nothing else was possible . . . She had sucked in with her mother's milk the profound truth that a woman's life is always a renunciation, greater or less.' She will face the future 'calmly and genially', 'be a good wife to the man whom, with all his excellences, she had never loved'. She gives £100 to Willie to start a new life in Australia: 'This vision of him was her stay.' In fact the young man was never heard of by anyone again. And here is the last sentence of Bennett, student of Zola and de Maupassant: 'The abandoned pitshaft does not deliver up its secret. And so—the Bank of England is the richer by a hundred pounds unclaimed, and the world the poorer by a simple and meek soul stung to revolt only in its last hour.'

There is good stuff in *Anna*—which for some unknown reason Bennett did not later like; he quoted with approval, or at any rate complacency, the comment of a reviewer: 'An entirely uninteresting tale about entirely uninteresting people', and even his friend H. G. Wells thought it 'a photograph a little out of focus'. It lacks Bennett's later skills, particularly those deployed in *Clayhanger* which in one way reworks some of the material—sisterly love, Methodist society, revivalist meetings, paternal tyranny. Yet it is crisp and vivid; set against what was to become in Bennett the almost routine, depressing description of industrial Staffordshire, there is a charmingly evoked idyllic interlude on the Isle of Man, with its splendid 'high teas' and comfortable lodgings, where for once two Methodists—Alderman and Mrs Sutton—are shown as generous and warm-hearted people.

'A mere lark', Bennett called *The Grand Babylon Hotel* (1902), published after three weeks evening work the same year as *Anna*. The 'lark' sold 50,000 hardback copies in the author's lifetime. It is thin stuff full of incredible and complicated mysteries, escapes, romance, foreign princes, millionaire Americans. It does, however, introduce the luxury hotel theme he exploited most effectively in *Imperial Palace*. He was fascinated by *hotels de luxe*, great stores and ocean liners, the people who worked in them and those who used them. Wealth was an element in their attraction for him, and in *Grand Babylon* we have a 'good' character, Prince Aribert, observing 'the value and the marvellous power of mere money, of the lucre philosophers pretend to despise and men sell their souls for'. Bennett himself, born poor, never doubted the marvellous power of mere money. Hotels, too, evoked in Bennett admiration for the complex organization lying behind them; he organized his best novels no less scrupulously. Strangely enough it was this ill-organized, insubstantial *Grand Babylon* that really put Bennett on the map; it was his first work to be reviewed in *The Times*.

As well as writing serials for the magazines, Bennett was producing short stories collected under such titles as *Tales of the Five Towns* (1905) and *The Grim Smile of the Five Towns* (1907). Most of the stories were not grim at all, but light, amusing, often ingenious if sometimes jocosely narrated. The latter collection contains his masterpiece in this genre, 'The Death of Simon Fuge'. Here the plot dwindles almost to nothing—merely visits from one house to another—and there are some close parallels, as Miss Drabble points out, with de Maupassant's, 'Le Rosier de Mme Husson'. Yet Bennett's story is no feeble imitation. The narrator, Loring, a porcelain expert on business from the British Museum, is visiting the Potteries for the first time. In the train from London he reads of the death of a distinguished if rather precious painter, Simon Fuge, whose origins were in the Potteries but whose reputation had been largely created in London. This reputation had been based upon his achievements, not only as a painter but as an impulsive amorist and a *raconteur*, and in particular upon his description of a romantic night in his youth with two beautiful sisters in a boat on a Staffordshire lake. Everything Loring sees as he descends from the train at Knype is, he thinks, 'a violent negation' of Simon Fuge, that 'entity of rare, fine, exotic sensibilities, that perfectly mad gourmet of sensations . . .'. What could such a creature have had to do with the dirt in the air, the brusque porter, the undersized potters, the advertisements for soap, boots and aperients?

Loring's host, an architect called Brindley, has heard of

Fuge but expects, rightly, that few others in the Potteries have. Brindley, highly knowledgeable, a man of positive views, even eccentric, is 'a very tonic dose'; his wife, capable and vivacious. Despite the mud and heavy vapour and glaring furnaces—'I do not think the Five Towns will ever be described: Dante lived too soon'—Loring finds himself among boisterously cultured people with not a pretension among them but with gusto and appetite for the new—and skill: Strauss's *Sinfonia Domestica*, then newly composed, is played from piano parts at sight. They eat with great appetite (including prawns in aspic—'it seemed strange to me to have crossed the desert of pots and cinders in order to encounter prawns in aspic': menus are often lovingly described in Bennett). Loring meets the two subjects of Fuge's romantic anecdotes—one now a barmaid, another the wife of a rich manufacturer who certainly remembers Fuge on the lake: he talked about neckties and his cold feet and they were back home from the lake by 11 p.m.—so much for the all night outing. Yet neither bathos nor the omnipresent irony are all that 'Simon Fuge' offers. Here is realism but lightly dealt with, an almost delicious confection, and what Bennett is saying with subtlety is that delight in the arts and in living exists among the 'pots and cinders', may indeed exist more vigorously and without the pretentiousness of great cities such as London and Paris. He is also doubtless saying that the prophet has no honour in his own country, as was for long Bennett's own experience.

The Old Wives' Tale (1908), unlike most of Bennett's serious fiction, has a theme, ancient, commonplace and yet new for every human being: Time, Mutability and Death. It has been expressed throughout history in a variety of ways—in nostalgia for the past, in the Elizabethan horror at the fact of physical dissolution, in the yearning of Wordsworth for the permanence of mountains and, more pertinently to *The Old Wives' Tale*, in Villon's *Ballade du Temps Jadis*, that poignant lament that even the grace and beauty of women should be subject to the destruction of time. The centre-pieces of the novel are two sisters whom we first meet as young girls—Constance pretty, plump and placid, and Sophia, darkly beautiful, ardent, and wayward. From their home over their parents' flourishing drapery shop in the square of a small Potteries town, we follow them through matrimony, disaster, death of relatives, some happiness, much compromise, to their physical decline and death. The gradual ageing of the sisters steals on them and us like a thief in the night, until some external fact, unobtrusively dropped into the narrative, reveals it. The novel's incidents are remarkably varied whether in Bursley, where Constance lives out her life, or in Paris, where Sophia spends thirty years of hers; and the comparatively trivial events of Bursley (though they do include a murder) have no less impact on Constance than have the more dramatic events in the life of Sophia, abandoned in Paris by the faithless, spendthrift Gerald, whom she married after her youthful, romantic fixation on him.

Though the two sisters occupy the centre of the stage, this book of 200,000 words is thickly peopled, with aunts, ancestors, and such apparently immortal persons as the thin, rasping chemist Critchlow, as harsh in voice as in character, the lover of disaster, ruthless, a carrion crow. No less interesting is the humble draper's assistant, Samuel Povey, who becomes Constance's loyal husband, and modernizes the shop. In Paris, we meet the charming French journalist, Chirac, who is kind to Sophia and then becomes so enamoured of her as to appear foolish—and Sophia 'could not admire weakness. He had failed in human dignity. And it seemed to her as if she had not previously been quite certain whether she could not love him, but that now she was quite certain.' The beautiful Sophia never loves again after her husband leaves her.

Servants, babies and dogs contribute to the rich variegation of the novel. In the days of which he wrote, even the lower middle classes could afford to employ what were in reality downtrodden maids-of-all-work. Maggie, big, gawky, charmless, is the most memorable. She has bossed Constance and Sophia as children; she is not badly treated, in the context of the time, but, says Bennett: 'She was what was left of a woman after twenty-two years in the cave [i.e. basement kitchen] of a philanthropic family.' Suddenly this 'dehumanized drudge' shows signs of 'capricious individuality' and marries the drunken fish-hawker. Towards the end of the book servants are harder to get and far less servile; such is the 'pretty and impudent' Maud, 'her gaze cruel, radiant and conquering . . . She knew she was torturing her old and infirm mistresses. She did not care. Her motto was: War on employers. Get all you can out of them, for they will get all they can out of you. On principle—the sole principle she possessed—she would not stay in a place more than six months.' How good too is Bennett with babies and children! Of him his friend, Marriott, said 'he loved little children and instantly won their affection.' With humour and imagination he takes us inside the little world of Constance's baby boy rolling on a shawl on the hearthrug conducting experiments—'chiefly out of idle amusement'—with a ball, a doll and Fan the dog:

> He rolled with a fearful shock, arms and legs in air, against the mountainous flank of that mammoth Fan, and clutched at Fan's ear. The whole mass of Fan upheaved and vanished from his view, and was instantly forgotten by him. . . . Terrific operations went on over his head. Giants moved to and fro. Great vessels were carried off and great books were brought and deep voices rumbled regularly in the spaces beyond the shawl. But he remained oblivious. . . . An uncomfortable sensation in his stomach disturbed him; he tolerated it for fifty years or so, and then he gave a little cry. Life has resumed its seriousness.

Dogs have a considerable role in several of Bennett's novels, and he has a rare ability to see the world from what is credibly their point of view. Spot, the fox terrier puppy of Constance's later years, has been washed: 'He was exquisitely soft to the touch and to himself he was loathsome. His eyes continually peeped forth between corners of the agitated towel, and they were full of inquietude and shame.' But it is the chocolate-coloured poodle, Fossette, cut in the French style, who has the chief canine role. We meet her first when Sophia has become the super-efficient proprietor of the best *pension* in Paris, and Fossette is a master's last touch to the portrait of Sophia's new *persona*. To Fossette goes the honour of the final sentences in the book when both her mistress and Constance are dead. By now the poodle, too, is old and lame. While Constance's funeral is taking place she feels upset in her habits and neglected. The maid, however, puts her dinner before her in the usual soup-plate. But Fossette, to show her *dérangement*, sniffs and walks away and lies down 'with a dog's sigh'. Then she reconsiders: 'She glanced at the soup-plate, and, on the chance that it might after all contain something worth inspection, she awkwardly balanced herself on her old legs and went to it again.' So the novel ends; so life goes on.

The *Tale* has its *longueurs* and its oddities: why for example does the author suddenly become 'I' once and once only (in referring to Samuel Povey)? But for all that, it is a true, created work of art. Its general movement, though varied in pace, is majestic and sure-footed; Book I is the opening statement with Constance and Sophia in their parents' home; Book II is the story of Constance after Sophia has eloped; Book III is the adventures of Sophia in France; and Book IV is the reuniting of the sisters after thirty years— where the modulations are, in musical terms, resolved. In the telling of the story, everything is prepared for; what at first looks like chance is author's cunning. A sentence is apparently casually dropped in, rather as detective story writers scatter clues; but in Bennett the casual sentence heralds a move forward in the tale and thus adds verisimilitude, for the reader says to himself, 'yes, I remember that!'

See how skilfully the elephant (in Book I, ch. iv) is used to activate great sections of the book. It is Wakes week in Bursley; a circus arrives; an elephant goes mad and has to be shot. It is carried away and laid out pending disposal. There is great excitement among the town folk who cut off tusks, feet and bits of flesh for souvenirs. Even Mrs Baines is consumed by curiosity, and, accompanied by Constance and Samuel Povey, leaves her husband, who has lain stricken for fourteen years, to the care of Sophia, then in her academic mood, who professes a complete lack of interest in elephants, alive or dead. The husband cannot be left alone since, if he slides down in bed, he cannot right himself. Sophia, however, on her way to his bedroom, glimpses the attractive Gerald Scales entering the shop, leaves her father briefly and, returning, finds him dead from asphyxia, in one of Bennett's hardest, casually brutal pages 'his head hanging, inverted near the floor . . . his mouth was open, and the tongue protruded between the black, swollen mucous lips; his eyes were prominent and coldly staring.' Critchlow, who has regarded the helpless John Baines as 'his property, his dearest toy,' is called, and harshly tells Sophia that she has killed her father. Her mother, herself smitten with guilt, sobs: 'If it had been anything else but that elephant!' Sophia, afflicted by remorse, gives up her pupil-teaching with Miss Chetwynd because her late father had opposed the idea and returns to work in the shop. Thus she has more chance to meet Scales, who is a commercial traveller, and with him in due time she elopes. In Paris, 250 pages later when Scales has abandoned her, she ponders sadly: 'All this because mother and Constance wanted to see the elephant and I had to go into father's room! I should never have caught sight of him from the drawing-room window!' Nor can it be by chance that one of the few things Sophia recalls from her experiences of the siege of Paris by the Prussians is that, so great was the food shortage, the elephants from the zoo were killed and eaten.

How much of the novel's action flows from that elephant! Even Bennett's observations on the disappearance of early Victorian England are evoked by the death of John Baines, itself precipitated by curiosity about the dead elephant. There is considerable correlating of changes in the main characters with changes in the outer world, as in the play, *Milestones*. For instance Victorian parental authority is severely shaken when Sophia refuses to take the spoonful of castor oil her mother prescribes. Since Sophia was born in 1848, this puts her challenge around 1862—rather early, by some social historians' accounts, for young girls to be crossing their parents. Again, towards the end of the book, there is an attempt to federate the Five Towns; seeing this as an attack on the old municipal liberties, Constance struggles from her sick-bed to vote. The effort is too much for her and causes her death. There is a parallel here with the death of her husband, Samuel. As she fights for freedom, so he fought for justice. Back and forth he goes to the prison where his once jolly cousin, Dan the baker and 'follower of Pan', is incarcerated for murdering his drunken, dirty wife—Dan 'the man who for thirty years had marshalled all his immense pride to suffer this woman, the jolly man who had laughed through thick and thin.' Despite Samuel's efforts, Dan is hanged and he himself dies of the pneumonia he has neglected in his efforts to prevent what he sees as a great wrong.

In this novel, there is neither melodrama nor sentimentality. The author is scarcely even sympathetic towards his characters, but he is deeply curious about them. He 'creates' them by means of his psychological penetration, his inventiveness: 'I never,' he once wrote, 'see a porter without giving him a hearth and a home and worries and a hasty breakfast.' At the same time he is detached. Though he may sometimes be facetious, at least he never overwrites, so that the vivid phrases when they come have a forceful realism. The sickening description of the filthy *cabinets de toilette* in the house of the courtesans rivals Swift's 'A Beautiful Young Nymph Going to Bed'. Striking, too, is Mme Foucault, the fat and fading courtesan abandoned by her young (and she fears last) lover who falls sobbing in the tawdry room with its red-shaded lamp, 'a shapeless mass of lace, frilled linen and corset . . . Her face . . . was horrible, not a picture but a palette; or like the coloured design of a pavement artist after a heavy shower . . . Her flesh seemed to be escaping at all ends from a corset strained to the utmost limit. And above her boots—she was still wearing dainty, high-heeled, tightly laced boots—the calves bulged suddenly out.' This is the woman first seen by Sophia in all her smartness in a restaurant with an admiring male retinue; the woman who, too, has tended her in her illness; but a woman incurably light and irresponsible, thus differing from Bennett's later courtesans who tend to have 'hearts of gold'.

French life, as seen by the disillusioned Sophia, is mainly distasteful and this offended Bennett's most perceptive critic, Georges Lafourcade, himself a Frenchman. To Sophia, France is a land of dirt, disorder and dishonesty, whose people crave for sensation such as seeing a man guillotined. This sight inflames the crowd, among whom Sophia, led by her wanton husband, finds herself, and incites it to orgies both alcoholic and sexual. With what nostalgia does she see at Messrs Cook's *bureau de change* 'a little knot of English people, with naïve, romantic and honest faces, quite different from the faces outside in the street. No corruption in those faces, but a sort of wondering and infantile sincerity, rather out of its element.' How admirable now to the once rebellious Sophia appear all the rigid rules she had found so repressive! She thinks of 'the honest workmanship, the permanence, the absence of pretence' of Bursley life. But once back in Bursley for good, and unable to persuade her sister to quit the grime for the salubrious air of Buxton Spa, she reverses: 'She pictured Paris as it would be that very morning—bright, clean, glittering; the neatness of the Rue Lord Byron, and the magnificent slanting splendour of the Champs Elysées. Paris had always seemed beautiful to her; but the life of Paris had not seemed beautiful to her. Yet now it did seem beautiful.' She even recalls 'a regular, placid beauty in her daily life there'. This contrast is a part of Bennett's design that Lafourcade did not understand. The point is that Sophia has a considerable capacity for deceiving herself, just as she had deceived herself over the glamour of Gerald Scales; this capacity, the reader notes, she has in a greater degree than her far less experienced sister. Constance, too, has to the very end a stronger will than her sister; she will not leave her old home and Sophia will not leave her. There in the square at Bursley they will end their days.

To Sophia, Bennett gives the final enunciation of the grand theme of Time, Mutability and Death. She looks down at the dead and withered body of the once handsome young husband she has not seen for thirty years:

He and she had once loved and burned and quarrelled in the glittering and scornful pride of youth. But time had burned them out. 'Yet a little while', she thought, 'and I shall be lying on a bed like that. And what shall I have lived for? What is the meaning of it?' The riddle of life itself was killing her, and she seemed to drown in a sea of inexpressible sorrow.

Constance's judgement is simpler. 'Well, that is what life is!' Some critics have disputed Constance's view. Henry

James asked, 'Yes, yes—but is this *all*?' And Walter Allen wrote: 'It misses greatness, if one believes that there is that in man which transcends time.' One might certainly make such criticisms of almost every other Bennett novel. Yet surely *The Old Wives' Tale*, though saying 'Yes, this *is* all,' raises the reader by means of its implacable hard look into what life has been for two women, and by a sort of catharsis, to a final calm and lofty contemplation of the unchangeable facts of life.

I think we may allow Bennett his mild boast: 'The effect as you finish the last page,' he wrote in a letter, 'is pretty stiff—*when you begin to think things over.*'

In the same year (1908) as *The Old Wives' Tale, Buried Alive* was published. Bennett referred to it as 'high class humour'. It is not particularly funny; though containing some farcical scenes, these are not what the reader specially enjoys. The far-fetched plot concerns a pathologically shy but very successful painter, Priam Farll, whom not even art-dealers have seen, and who seizes the opportunity of the sudden death of his 'man', Leek, to swop identities.[1] Leek is buried as Priam Farll in Westminster Abbey (Farll attends the occasion of his own burial and bursts into uncontrollable tears); Farll then meets and marries the woman, Alice Challice, whom Leek had been pursuing through a matrimonial agency. The comfy Alice, shrewd, innocent, patient and practical, is the great creation of the book: 'She was the comfortablest cushion of a creature' and, in the last sentence of the book, Priam travels to 'a sweet exile with the enchantress Alice'. Previously they lived happily together in a painstakingly accurately depicted Putney of the era. When Farll, driven by the urge to paint which is his *raison d'être*, starts painting again, Alice humours him and is triumphant at selling his pictures for £5 each to a local shop. She is duly astonished when a sleek art-dealer, Mr Oxford, having recognized the style of Leek as authentically that of Farll, offers him what to Alice are incredible prices. Then comes a court case over Farll's alleged bigamy. Alice performs coolly and devastatingly in the witness box. The case

---

[1] Bennett may have remembered that J. M. W. Turner lived for ten years under the assumed name of Booth.

successfully over, the unlikely couple sail off together to Algiers.

Farll is one of the few really credible painters in fiction. A fool, perhaps 'but never a fool on canvas. He said everything there and said it to perfection.' Bennett had been friendly with real artists in their studios in Paris, and was himself a moderate water colourist; he as well as Farll 'knew —none better—that there is no satisfaction save the satisfaction of fatigue after honest endeavour . . .'. Once accept the improbabilities, the reader can scarcely not succumb to this unique novel.

Bennett lacked flair in entitling his novels. *Clayhanger* (1910) for instance, is not exactly guaranteed to attract the stray reader: its sound is leaden, it breathes the atmosphere of a bog. The book itself seems bowed down beneath its 130,000 words. But the reader who ventures upon it will quickly forget the title, which is the surname of the chief character, Edwin; and, once into it, may find it all too short.

The young Edwin, shy, sensitive and attracted by architecture and painting, is the son of Darius, another of Bennett's family tyrants. Once more, most of the action takes place in the Potteries, of which we are treated to yet another description. Darius is master of a small printing firm, whose work is minutely described. His life has been hard and he insists that Edwin, at first reluctant, follow him in his business in which he later becomes genuinely interested. The young Edwin is at odds (or would be if he could conquer his weakness and indecision) with almost everyone—his sisters, the artificially emotional Auntie Hamps, himself— and everything. Through him, Bennett directs a blast at the deficiencies of the education of the day, at what he sees as the boredom and hypocrisy of Wesleyan Methodism about which he is coldly sarcastic, and at the ugliness and provincialism of the Potteries and its class consciousness.

But then *Clayhanger* changes from being a near-sociological tract (with occasional lumps of sheer history) into a psychological novel. Sex, naturally, has been a worry to Edwin, inhibited no less by his nature than by his times and place. Sex—though in no very explicit terms since Bennett wished to sell to a wide public—is presaged in one of the most brilliant chapters Bennett wrote. Called 'Free and Easy' it describes 'a jollity of the Bursley Mutual Burial Club' (a sardonic touch) at the Dragon pub to which Edwin accompanies his father's giant chief compositor, Big James. Among the entertainments is Florence, the clog dancer with short red-and-black velvet skirts and 'complete visibility of her rounded calves'. As her finale she throws one foot as high as her head: 'Edwin was staggered. The blood swept into his face, a hot tide . . .' Sexual relations—or relations between the sexes—are the main subject of *Clayhanger* and of its two sequels, *Hilda Lessways* and especially of *These Twain*. When Edwin first meets Hilda, he thinks her rather abrupt and unfeminine, though he is struck by her intelligence and strong personality and that kind of waywardness the young Sophia had. Then he falls in love with her despite (or because of) her somewhat mysterious background, and the fact that she 'had unfathomable grottoes in her soul'. Unfathomable indeed! For, after exchanging love letters and tokens of affection, Edwin learns that Hilda has married another man (the how and why is explained in *Hilda Lessways*). She and her relationship with Edwin are full of swiftly-changing contradictions: 'From one extreme he flew to the other' in his view of her. In the third of the trilogy, *These Twain*, Bennett shows with great skill the progression of domestic antagonism and how each incident of estrangement is ended by a kiss. This divorce of sexual love from differences of opinion and downright quarrelling baffles Edwin: 'The heat of their kisses had not cooled; but to him at any rate the kisses often seemed intensely illogical . . . he had not yet begun to perceive that those kisses were the only true logic of their joint career.' So sexual love smoothes the way from differences to compromises; the trilogy admirably delineates the subtle interweaving not so much of love and hate as of passion and irritation. Bennett had not studied Stendhal in vain. 'Some women' says Gerald in *The Old Wives' Tale*, 'only enjoy themselves when they're terrified.' From masochism Bennett turns in *Clayhanger* to sadism: 'As he looked at the wet eyes and shaken bosom of Hilda Cannon, he was aware of acute joy. Exquisite moment! Damn her! He could have taken her and beaten her in his sudden passion—a passion not of revenge, not of punishment! He could have made her scream with the pain that his love would inflict.' Such observations were uncommon in popular English fiction of that day. *Clayhanger* and its sequels are, however, just as much about a shy young man who becomes a success in business and of a woman, particularly in *Hilda Lessways* who, like Wells's Ann Veronica, makes her own way in the wider world then still largely reserved for men.

Bennett had no very high opinion of *The Card* (1911): 'Stodgy, no real distinction of any sort, but well invented and done up to the knocker, technically,' he wrote in his Journal; yet it is today the Bennett story best known to the wider public. The novel narrates the rise of Denry Machin from rent collector in the Five Towns to fortune and high municipal honours. He is joker, opportunist, not invariably truthful (though he never tells lies 'save in the greatest crises'), a buccaneer with his heart in the right place. As Lafourcade noted, however, Denry is not naturally audacious; he is fundamentally shy. But he has an iron will which triumphs and turns him into a local legend. The narrative goes with great verve and is written with a curious double irony—two tongues in cheek. It is full of ingenious and comic invention, as in the incident when Denry's mule drawing the carriage containing the Duchess of Chell refuses to move at the sight of squads of policemen drawn up to welcome their distinguished visitor. There are some amusing descriptions, for example of the recently knighted local philanthropist: 'Even before the bestowal of the knighthood his sense of humour had been deficient and immediately afterwards it had vanished entirely. Indeed, he did not miss it.' Bennett creates some well-observed secondary characters such as the clerk, Penkethman, and Denry's masterful and obstinate mother. Bennett, seeing the popularity of *The Card*, continued Denry's story in *The Regent* (1913) in which he becomes a London theatrical impresario; it lacks some of the bounce and *brio* of *The Card* but it is entertaining enough.

Though Bennett wrote a great deal during the 1914–18 war, not until *The Pretty Lady* (1918) did he publish a novel of note. This was yet another departure, and it had successors in the Bennett canon. Since the novel largely concerns a French *cocotte* in wartime London, it was described in the press correctly as pornographic (writing about a harlot) but incorrectly as unsavoury, wallowing in the slime of sensuality, decadent and so on. This ensured excellent sales—20,000 in the first month. Bennett had always been intrigued by the *secrets d'alcôve* as was noted above. Professional sex-providers also interested him. In his *Paris Nights* sketches (1913) he observes that 'some of the odalisques are beautiful. Fine women in the sight of heaven! They too are experts with the preoccupation of experts, they are at work and this is the battle of life. They inspire respect.' This was not prurience, but rather that admiration for professionalism which he had earlier shown in describing the work of skilled printers and potters. At the same time, with his keen journalistic nose, he had sniffed out that the war, with its horrors and sudden death, had loosened restraints. As Christine, heroine of *The Pretty Lady*, says: 'The war in London has led to the discovery that men have desires.' Needless perhaps to say, Bennett treated the physical side of Christine's profession discreetly though with calm realism, as in the description of the five great plagues to which she and her colleagues are subject. Physical sex comes over atmospherically, not explicitly. Bennett did not need or want as an artist the crude explicitness permitted (indeed demanded) in the 1970s; he was far from wishing to imitate the semi-mystical and essentially asexual frenzies described by his younger contemporary, D. H. Lawrence. Nor was Bennett especially influenced (whatever that means) by Goncourt's *La Fille Elisa*, Balzac's *Grandeurs et Misères des Courtisanes* or Zola's *Nana*. He simply wanted to write about the gamut of relationships between men and women. In *The Pretty Lady* he writes not only about the religious *cocotte* Christine but also about the sexual nature of the war widow, Concepcion, and of the aristocratic, sensation-seeking, neurotic Lady Queenie. Christine's life is presented as healthy, Queenie's as morbid. The hero (if such he is) of the book is one of Christine's clients, G. J. Hoape, the well-to-do, intelligent, self-possessed bachelor. Jealousy of

Christine leads him to the wrong conclusion about her as is revealed in the last few pages. The ending is a surprise, but this is no spurious denouement; the reader will admit that Bennett has more than adequately prepared him for it, far more adequately perhaps than he had done in the shock ending of *Anna of the Five Towns* sixteen years earlier. The war as reflected in London is a big element in *The Pretty Lady*—the drunken officer she succours, the leave train departing, the vividly pictured air raid, even the wartime committee meetings. The war is thought of by G. J. Hoape as 'a vast dark moving entity'. The novel does not quite cohere, yet even these loose ends convey the disjointedness of life in wartime London.

Lilian (1922), the story of a poor but pretty young middle-class typist who runs away to the south of France with her middle-aged employer, is a sort of bridge to such later, better works as *Lord Raingo* and *Imperial Palace*. After the workaday early part, Bennett launches into the world of luxury hotels, dancing, cards, fine food, *trains de luxe*—the world of *Imperial Palace*. The middle-aged hero, Felix, is a stage along the road from Hoape to Raingo. In a small role, there is a kindly French prostitute. In a sense the poor but well brought up Lilian herself has to choose, as Bennett points out, between starvation and prostitution; in becoming Felix's mistress she chooses what might be regarded as the latter. However, when she is pregnant, Felix marries her and shortly dies from pneumonia. Lilian, now a rich widow, returns to take over her husband's home from his middle-aged spinster sister—and there in his bedroom she has never seen before, she suddenly feels the damped-down emotion of her loss. She reacts in a strange, yet markedly Bennettian way. She picks up one of her husband's neckties, 'bit it passionately, voluptuously; the feel of the woven stuff thrilled her . . . Lilian sobbed like a child.' Yet Lilian is never less than 'a nice girl' (she is shocked at being taken as one of 'us girls' by the prostitute). Matter-of-factness, irony, even gentle cynicism—and a certain carelessness—imbue the book. I do not think Bennett was seeking to emulate the then popular 'problem' novels and plays of which Galsworthy's are the best examples; but there *is* a problem raised

33

in *Lilian*—how wise is it for a pretty young girl to marry a middle-aged man? He can indeed provide a happier life, exercise a more beneficial influence, if he is well disposed, than most impecunious young men of her own age—and Lilian is delighted to be seen dancing with Felix; but sooner rather than later she is likely to be a heart-broken still youngish widow. At least she will be well off. The problem perhaps reflects Bennett's own.

Mr Prohack, also published in 1922, is about an upper civil servant who has saved the Treasury millions during the war while his own income has remained stationary. He is left a large legacy by a war profiteer; multiplies it by investment; and suffers from boredom and nervous ailments because he cannot find anything satisfying on which to spend his money. Eventually, he buys a paper-making business. The novel is about the rich and riches and it is not very good; yet Prohack himself—kindly, humorous, epigrammatic and resigned—is as interesting a character as any in Bennett's minor novels.

The stream of minor, sometimes trivial, novels and stories did not cease, but they were interrupted in the mid-1920s by three works of higher calibre. The first was *Riceyman Steps* (1923) which was hailed on all sides as a major creation, Conrad remarking 'this is Bennett triumphant,' Wells 'a great book . . . as good as or better than *The Old Wives' Tale*'; and for it Bennett received the first literary prize of his career, the James Tait Black. It must, however, be said at the outset that *Riceyman Steps* is, overall, as gloomy as Strindberg and set entirely in a grimy bookseller's shop in Clerkenwell, one of the dingiest areas in London. It is a book entirely without hope; but it also lacks the perspective that in *The Old Wives' Tale*, at the end after all the sadness, lifts the reader to a loftier plane. Few readers can want to return, at any rate quickly, to a second reading of *Riceyman Steps*; it may be admired, it can scarcely be loved. Of a story-line there is even less trace than usual in Bennett's serious novels. All that happens, George Moore said, was that 'a bookseller crosses the road to get married'. This is not quite fair; nevertheless it has, to an even greater degree than elsewhere, that motionlessness noted above. As Lafourcade puts it, Bennett here carried his technique—of the casual mention of a fact which subsequently becomes an important clue—to extremes: 'One feels that if the author were put on his mettle, he could write half a dozen chapters, perhaps half a dozen novels, merely to explain why one of his heroes blew his nose with his left hand, or had a wart over his right eye.'

Earlforward, the antiquarian bookseller, looked after by a goodhearted buxom young charwoman, Elsie, is a miser. He marries a widow, Violet, who has been left some money and who appears to be at least thrifty. Both subsequently die, in part at least because of Earlforward's meanness. A miser—yes, but Earlforward is a true original. He is not a Darius; nor is he Shylock, Volpone or Harpagon. He is a kind, patient, bland and rather lazy man; with a little more effort he could make much more money. Moreover, he genuinely and sensually loves his Violet. Yet, as she sees it, 'He was in love with her, but he was more in love with his grand passion and vice, which alone had power over him and of which he, the bland tyrant over all else, was the slave.' He is a Jekyll and Hyde figure, a basically amiable man seized by a dreadful psychological disease, just as cancer physically seizes him in the end. Bennett rather overdoes his actual worship of real gold: 'Nothing like it!' he said blandly, running his fingers through the sovereigns that tinkled with elfin music.' This somewhat artificial, Jonsonian image, however, triggers off Violet's more subtle reactions: 'She was astounded, frightened, ravished . . . He was a superman, the most mysterious of supermen.' Thinking of the magic gold she calls him importunately to bed; he obeys. There Bennett's psychological penetration is superb; but when in a further attempt to stress the nature of Earlforward's disease he has him inquire of the man in charge of the vacuum-cleaning machines: 'Do you sell the dirt? Do you get anything for it?', the effect is merely ludicrous.

Violet, Earlforward's wife, though she has some resemblance to Alice Challice, is not much developed; her main function is to act as a catalyst. Nevertheless, like some other Bennett women, she is shown as loving and hating simultaneously: 'She hated him; her resentment against him was very keen, and yet she wanted to fondle him, physically and spiritually.' A subtler portrait is that of Elsie, the unselfish young char, a war widow of twenty-three, who is both loyal and shy; yet in her hunger she can steal; though chaste she is sensuous; and will take matters into her own hands when she thinks fit, not least when a former admirer, Joe, turns up, ill and unkempt. But Elsie is insufficient to alleviate the gloom that in the end permeates the novel and is what we remember of it.

Curiously enough, *Lord Raingo* (1926), to the dying of whose eponymous hero some 200 pages are accorded, is not a gloomy book and it is far fuller of incident than its predecessor. The basic story, however, is not complicated. Sam Raingo, millionaire, and once an undistinguished MP, is called by the wartime Prime Minister and his boyhood friend, Andy Clyth, to be Minister of Records (a cover name for propaganda) towards the end of the first World War. He accepts—so long as he is given a title and, because of his health, is not required to fight elections and cosset constituents. Part of the novel is devoted to the political manœuvrings which persist in governments, however huge the front-line casualties become. The manœuvrings wash around Sam himself, because he is popular and because he has renounced any salary; but he stoutly defeats them. Sam, like Andy Clyth, is a master of what Bennett calls 'chicane'; a shrewd man who sees with a sure instinct the inner meaning of acts and remarks. The novel contains much not very covert biography; Clyth with his ruthless subtlety and his Celtic 'poetry' is Lloyd George, and his personal secretary, Rosie Packer, who 'rules the Empire', is Frances Stevenson, later the Countess Lloyd George. The belligerent Minister of Munitions, Tom Hogarth, was modelled on Winston Churchill (as the latter insouciantly recognized). Doubtless other of the novel's Ministers are near-portraits of real persons; much of Bennett's information about the procedures involved in becoming a Lord and about ministerial function came from his friend, Lord Beaverbrook. Bennett is closer here than anywhere to the *roman à clef*. Raingo himself has certain of Bennett's characteristics—his passion for punctuality and his gaily-coloured bow-ties (which are nearly Raingo's downfall); Bennett did briefly become non-ministerial head of the Ministry of Information. There is, however, much in Raingo, as in G. J. Hoape and Felix, which is clearly not Bennett.

Raingo loves being a Lord, loves running—and efficiently —a department, loves being recognized not least by the press. Once more, Bennett scatters clues. In the novel's beginning is foreshadowed Raingo's end. The reader is casually warned that Raingo has a hypochondriac mania for doctors. The fact is, however, that this middle-aged, successful, comfortable man, really does have a dubious heart, result of infantile rheumatic fever. We wonder uneasily whether he is going to die; we are never quite sure that he will until he does. His prolonged illness, its phases and treatments so minutely described, need not necessarily be fatal. Incidentally, Bennett must surely have recalled this fictional death-bed when he himself lay ill for some weeks preceding his death in 1931; his death, too, was due to 'a bit of carelessness' as was Raingo's; doubtless, too, he exhibited all the sick Raingo's suspiciousness.

Raingo has a wife Adela, another original creation. She is vague, self-absorbed, upper-class ('she had race'), tepid, nonchalant—so nonchalant indeed that in moments of marital intimacy, she makes such remarks as 'I wonder where I left my umbrella this afternoon'. They have one son, a prisoner-of-war. Not surprisingly, Raingo has a mistress, Delphine, a young woman of voluptuous charms; not a courtesan but a poor, kind girl, whom he rescued from poverty. But, like G. J. Hoape, he is suspicious of her; suspicion—or insight—plays a considerable part in his life. Though Delphine is always loving towards him, he thinks she is playing him false. Bennett cleverly works up the tension until at last Raingo catches sight of her with a young officer at the Savoy. She was once engaged to the young man, and broke it off. By accident she meets him again when he is on leave from the Western Front. Naturally she is kind to him, though as her sister, Gwen, a pretty bus conductress, explains, kind 'in a nice way if you knows what I mean. Oh yes, it was all *right*.' Delphine, however, is tormented by doubt: he is at the Front; ought she not to stick by him even though she does not care for him? On top of all that, after the death of Raingo's wife in a car accident, Raingo proposes marriage to her and this exacerbates her mental torment. She disappears. It is the sick Raingo who spots in a small newspaper paragraph the report of a nameless girl found dead below the cliffs at Brighton; with his unerring instinct he knows it is she, and she it is. Raingo has loved Delphine; he thinks of 'enchanted moments' with her; yet in his last minutes of life, 'He murmured appealingly in the final confusion of his mind: "Adela!" His jaw fell.' Adela is his dead wife's name. As with the shock surprises at the end of *Anna of the Five Towns* and of *The Pretty Lady*, the reader accepts the shock, not as an O. Henry trick,[1] but as a revelation of a psychological truth.

Raingo is immensely self-conscious, self-analytical and no less controlled than his author; capable of malice, even of cynicism, but in non-aggressive ways. A man whose 'sturdy rationalism' could admit that 'Rationalism was as dogmatic as mysticism and superstition'. And he is surrounded by cleverly delineated characters—Trumbull, Mrs Blacklow (who is pregnant two years after her husband became a POW), the pompous Timmerson, and the General who seeks to do Raingo down: thumbnail sketches, but vivid. Add to them the idiosyncratic physician, the subtly differentiated nurses and Mayden, Raingo's confidant who in peacetime runs a chain of hotels, in whom perhaps we have a preliminary sketch of Evelyn Orcham, the Managing Director of *Imperial Palace*. The novel has flaws: *would* Delphine be so tortured by the choice before her that she would commit suicide? Would there be an immediate affinity between Geoffrey Raingo, the ex-POW son of Raingo, and Gwen, sister of Delphine; is there not too much coincidence (too much at any rate for fiction) in Geoffrey, twisted with neurosis, arriving home as his mother's funeral cortège passes by? These are small matters: Lafourcade is surely right in ranking *Lord Raingo* 'immediately below the masterpieces'.

[1] O. Henry (1862–1910), American writer of short stories, all of them notable for the surprising unexpectedness of their endings.

Imperial Palace (1930) is the longest—243,000 words—and last of his novels, save for the unfinished *A Dream of Destiny*. It is almost but not quite a 'documentary', exposing to the reader in technical detail—as Bennett had done with a draper's shop and a printing works—every corner of the workings and organization of the 'grand' hotel, as typical a creation of late Victorian times as the luxury liner and the Pullman carriage. Before the grand hotel existed, the titled and rich stayed with a retinue of servants in hired villas or the palaces of friends; the discriminating middle class preferred 'lodgings'. These grand hotels were possibly temporary phenomena; today they are used mainly by rich actors and passing expense-account businessmen. They had always fascinated Bennett, who, when young, once wrote that his secret ambition had been to be the manager of a grand hotel. Today surely an inconceivable ambition for such as Bennett! Then, however, for an impecunious young man from the Potteries, who did not believe in God, it was the temple of his substitute God, luxury, to which he could aspire if only as an acolyte. Of course to write a novel about such an obsession required a rationale: he provided it. Observing that his earlier *Grand Babylon Hotel* was a mere lark, he went on (in his Journal for 25 September 1929): 'The big *hotel de luxe* is a very serious organization; it is in my opinion a unique subject for a serious novel; it is stuffed with human nature of extremely various kinds. The subject is characteristic of the age; it is as modern as the morning's milk; it is tremendous and worthy of tremendous handling.'

Lafourcade claims that the hotel itself, redolent to Bennett of romance and beauty and superb intricate organization, is the real hero of the novel. This is not true; a novel cannot exist without human beings (Virginia Woolf's *The Waves* is scarcely a novel), and only a specialist researcher would read *Imperial Palace* to find out how the London Savoy was run in the 1920s. Though Bennett claims that the novel has 'eighty-five speaking characters' (the figure has been disputed), there are really only three of great account: the precise, reserved, super-efficient, long widowed and celibate Evelyn Orcham, Managing Director of the *Imperial Palace*. The second is Gracie Savott, daughter of a millionaire, the sophisticated, talented, untidy, capricious, sensation-seeking woman of the 1920s, akin to Lady Queenie and in a different context Hilda Lessways, and to society women of the day. Gracie, for example, 'adores' something because it is so awful; this 'liking for ugliness', morbidity of taste, was part of the period that went in for primitive carvings and such perverseness of conduct as portrayed in Aldous Huxley and D. H. Lawrence's *Women in Love*. Nor can Bennett forbear the social comment on Gracie: 'Idle, luxurious, rich, but a masterpiece! Maintained in splendour by the highly skilled and expensive labour of others, materially useless to society, she yet justified herself by her mere appearance. And she knew it, and her conscience was clear.'

Gracie determines to seduce Evelyn, mainly because she only ever wants somebody who seems not especially to want her. She succeeds—in one of those ghastly Parisian furnished flats *de convenance* such as Bennett had portrayed in *The Old Wives' Tale*—and once more there are hints of perversities. When the affair is ended by Gracie, Evelyn ponders:

A whip might keep her in order. . . . What I ought to do is to go back with a cane and rip everything off her, and give her a hiding until she fainted away, and then, when she came to, make her kneel down and beg my pardon for being thrashed.

The seduction scenes in Paris are demure by present-day criteria yet in them Bennett went further than ever before— he knew precisely what the 1920s would tolerate—with talk of 'sumptuous breasts', kissing 'her open mouth', shameless visions in the bath, Gracie's appearances in knickers and camisole only. And the plain statement that she was not a virgin. The actual sexual encounters are, however, done by hint not description. Nevertheless, Bennett was kicking over the traces: he even briefly introduces two Lesbians fondling each other at a night club. There are other themes in the Evelyn–Gracie relationship: the struggle for mastery, the curious playing at home-making.

The third personage of moment is Violet Powler, whom Evelyn transfers from the hotel laundry to the post of head housekeeper. She is a sensible, even prim girl who deals admirably with the staff, not least with one of the hotel managers; by contrast with Gracie she is more than a little dull and submissive. Yet Evelyn comes to see her as 'all woman . . . challenging and very feminine'. They have a tiff, but this only increases her 'passion for the welfare and efficiency of the Palace'. She has determination (she saves the grill room manager who absented himself for some days), and she is ladylike (Evelyn is agreeably assured by a 'gentleman'), intelligent without education, energetic. So he marries her. She is in fact a superior Alice Challice of *Buried Alive*. The other characters are foils either to the hotel theme or less often to the romantic theme: old Dennis Dover, the chairman of the hotel group, is sketched entertainingly enough, so is Long Sam the doorman, Immerson the publicity agent, and of course the Napoleonic millionaire, father of Grace, Sir Henry Savott, who precipitates the hotel merger, which is an important part of the novel's action. With him, Evelyn has a revealing conversation about underdogs. Says Evelyn: 'When I think for instance of you in your suite, or me here, and then of some of the fellows and girls down in the basements, I get a sort of notion that there must be something wrong somewhere.' Here Bennett is being haunted by his various Maggies in their kitchen 'caves'. In the past he had seen no justification for their sordid servitude, but now Savott puts some points which Evelyn (and Bennett) seem to accept. Savott says: 'When there are no underdogs the world will have to come to an end, because there won't be anything to improve. Perfection's another name for death, isn't it? . . .' Machinery is replacing the underdog, doing away with dirty, greasy, soul-destroying labour. True, the former bottle-washers now unemployed and their families may die of starvation and will continue to do so for a generation or two. But 'there is a chance that mass production and machinery will abolish the underdog altogether. There's no other chance. So in the sacred cause of social progress I am determined to bear with fortitude the present and future misfortunes of your underdogs.'

Imperial Palace, which incidentally started a fashion that continues to this day for novels set in hotels, is not a great work; it has dull passages and the hotel details may bore some readers; there are inconsistencies of style; and the narrative tails away. Yet as a whole it remains what library subscribers called 'a good read'.

IV. PLAYS

Throughout his writing life, Bennett toyed with the theatre; toyed is the word, for he seldom spent more than three weeks on writing a play. He wrote twenty or so, of which four are adaptations of his novels. Unlike Henry James, however, he did have a few genuine successes; from *Milestones* (1912), written in collaboration with Edward Knoblock, he made real money. All his plays, as Lafourcade acutely discerned, were by-products of his fictional writing.

What the Public Wants (1909) is a lively commentary on the sensational press, then in its early days, and on the *avant-garde* theatre. It poses the far from new conflict between good taste and giving the public what it wants, between idealism and making money; and comes to no profound conclusion. The central figure, the millionaire newspaper proprietor, Sir Charles Worgan, loses his fiancée but is far from losing the battle. The play is a comedy with just a touch of bitterness here and there, with irony and even epigrams. The newspaper office scenes and particularly Worgan's bright ideas for stimulating sales have lost none of their contemporaneity. He himself is ruthless, but not without a kindly heart; nor is he based at first hand on any newspaper mogul of the day, since Bennett at that time had never met one. Part of the play is set in Bursley—where else?—whence the Worgan family come. Sir Charles's brother, Francis, the wanderer who becomes a drama critic, observes of his critic colleagues: 'We've almost all of us come from the provinces, and we try to forget it . . . We don't even *read* about the provinces, except occasionally in *Bradshaw*.'[1]

Milestones covers in three acts the fortunes of a family from 1860 to 1912 and is mainly about what is now called the generation gap—or, like *The Old Wives' Tale*, about grow-

[1] *Bradshaw's Railway Almanack*, a standard railway timetable of the period.

ing old, and, subtly observed, the change it makes in character. When it was first performed on 5 March 1912, it had a cast which, later at any rate, would have been regarded as 'glittering' including—and here too is a generation gap for the modern reader—such about-to-be celebrities as Mary Jerrold, Lionel Atwill, Owen Nares and Gladys Cooper. The play, if sombre at heart, is often flippant, witty and amusing. Today it has that sort of period flavour—typists and iron-clad ships, the vogue for Ouida and the bicycle were then innovations—which would make it a successful revival on television or the stage; and it is linked with national events of the time, a conception developed by Noel Coward in *Cavalcade*.

The third play, worth at least a reading, is *The Title* (1918). It also is in part concerned with newspapers and it has plenty of amusing dialogue about the young daughter of the wartime Treasury Director of Accounts, who under the guise of writing cookery articles is really the trenchant anti-Government columnist Sampson Straight, who has recently attacked the system of Honours. Her mother is not without an epigrammatic gift: 'I stand in queues for hours because my servants won't—it's the latest form of democracy.' However the play really revolves round the question of Honours, doubtless put into Bennett's mind by the questionable behaviour of the then Prime Minister, Lloyd George, though the Honours scandal came later. The Treasury Director, Culver, has been offered a baronetcy. His view however, is that governments offer Honours to survive, to 'placate certain interests, influence votes and obtain secret funds . . . Honours are given to save the life of the Government.' Of course the List must be skilfully done: 'with about five or six decent names you can produce the illusion that after all the List is really rather good'. He wants no part of it. The drama of *The Title* amounts to this: Culver's wife has wondered how anyone could accept a title. Immediately it is offered to her husband, she changes her mind. He must accept. There follows an endearing scene of caresses, of intra-marital diplomatic finessing, then of wifely fury, of separate rooms: the wife wins—only to face the opposition of her children. Events become complex, even farcical; but at least they evoke two political *mots*. Says Mrs Culver: 'I consider all politics extremely silly. There never were any in my family, nor in your father's . . .' Her husband says with fine cynicism: 'No enlightened and patriotic person wants the Government to fall. All enlightened and patriotic persons want the Government to be afraid of falling. There you have the whole of war politics in a nutshell.' Few will claim that, standing alone, Bennett's plays would get more than a few lines in theatrical history. As part of his *opus* they are worth note—and are never less than readable.

V. OTHER WRITINGS

There is a whole group of Bennett's non-fictional writings which the reader will lose nothing by ignoring. Such are, for instance, *How to Live on 24 Hours a Day* (1907) or *Self and Self-Management* (1918). In them are trumpeted forth such bombast as 'Big, strong vital thinking is contained in these pages—thoughts that make a man reach up to his highest self.' Here Bennett speaks like a mixture of Emile Coué and Samuel Smiles, a hot-gospeller of the self. Elsewhere in his collections of articles his novelistic insight reasserts itself: he is sensible enough on such matters as relations between men and women—*The Plain Man and his Wife* (1913) is quite excellent—though too frequently he falls into platitude. His travel sketches such as *Paris Nights* (1913) and *Mediterranean Scenes* (1928) are bright and fresh, while such early books as *Journalism for Women* (1898) are full of genuinely practical advice; so is the didactic manual *How to Become an Author* (1903).

Some of Bennett's non-fictional by-products are too enjoyable to skip; the autobiographical *The Truth About an Author* (1903), the Journals and the Letters. The first of these is highly entertaining and so down-to-earth as to have caused offence, not indeed to the generality of readers, but to those critics of the day—they are still about—who sought to appear omniscient, leaning over the gold bar of heaven to address the mere mortals below. They would never have exposed themselves as did Bennett, revealing his reaction to the early spurning of his free-lancing efforts: 'I used to retire to my room with rejected stuff as impassive as a wounded Indian . . . Mere vanity always did and always will prevent me from acknowledging a reverse at the moment: not until I have retrieved my position can I refer to my discomfiture.' Worse was the awful 'truth' he vouchsafed about reviewing: how neither he nor any competent reviewer needs to read a book all through to know its quality and in any case regular reviewers are paid insufficient to make it worthwhile. Bennett writes that he gave as much brain-power and time as an article demanded—'up to the limit of his pay in terms of hours at ten shillings apiece. But each year I raise my price per hour.' Naturally, if he is writing purely for the advancement of his artistic reputation, he ignores finance and does it for 'glory alone'. He is just as open about his motive in writing his serial novels, some, though not all, of which are painfully third rate. He began by being determined to keep the 'novel-form unsullied for the pure exercise of the artist in me'. This went by the board 'the instant I saw a chance of earning the money of shame'. Such bravado did not please all his professional readers.

Bennett's Journals, at least in early days when he had little idea of publication, only aspiration, are less bold-as-brass; he confesses to doubting whether he could write at all. He feels in 1896 his inferiority to, as it happens, J. M. Barrie, 'a lack of bigness, and a presence of certain littlenesses'. The Journals, however, are among his very best productions; when he died they contained about one million words of which only 400,000 have been printed, partly because of possible offence, legal and otherwise, to some then still alive. A fuller version is now called for. The Journals are full of his ravening curiosity about people and places; about himself and his neuralgias, migraines and sleeplessness, his pleasure in clothes and new books, about his work as *Woman* editor; about his reading which, ranging from Beaumont and Fletcher to Cellini and most of the nineteenth-century French novelists, was clearly wider in scope than he afterwards professed; and about the inspiration and birth of his work—these sections are worthy to be compared with the Notebooks of Henry James. Literary historians will always study the Journals for Bennett's impressions of Wells, Conrad, Maugham, Frank Harris, Gissing, James, Shaw, Walpole and for the whole ambience of the literary world of his day. Social historians will consult them for Bennett's impressions of, for example, hotels (the Strand Palace in 1909 cost 10s. 6d. a day for bed and all meals), of the *risquée* comédienne Marie Lloyd, John Burns, the early Socialist, and for such unlikely remarks, when war broke out in 1914, as: 'I agree that Russia is the real enemy, and not Germany.' Later came references to Beaverbrook, Diana Manners (later Cooper), and all the notabilities of the post-war social whirl and political worlds. Good gossip, to put it at its lowest.

Bennett in his last five years was best known to the English world at large as a weekly contributor on literary subjects to the London *Evening Standard*, which on Thursdays, when his causerie appeared, actually rose in circulation. Most of these pieces were not strictly reviews of new books.[1] Years before, between 1908 and 1911, he had had a practice run for this kind of thing in A. R. Orage's *New Age*; a selection of these contributions had been collected in *Books and Persons* (1917). There, with discriminating gusto, he introduced the English public at large to Turgenev, Dostoevsky and Chekhov. He also delivered himself of the observation that 'Art is not the whole of life, and to adore musical comedy is not a crime.' It was typical of his unstuffy approach; it ensured that he would be denigrated by the monomaniac *littérateurs* of his day.

Just as he educated the Edwardian public to appreciate previously unknown literary delights, so in his *Standard* column fifteen years later, he spotted and made irresistible such unknowns as Faulkner, Hemingway, Graham Greene, Evelyn Waugh, Henry Williamson and Ivy Compton-Burnett. All proved worthy of the early boost Bennett gave them. He made best-sellers of L. Feuchtwanger's *Jew Süss* and Axel Munthe's *The Story of San Michele*—and some others which are properly forgotten now. He put his oar in on such matters as censorship, book prices, bookshops and

[1] All are now available in *Arnold Bennett: The Evening Standard Years*, Edited by A. Mylett, 1974.

theatres. Bennett was not a profound critic nor did he pretend to be one. His snap judgements however, were infrequently astray. He could be hard hitting; he seldom failed to entertain for, as he said, of a reviewer, 'unless he is interesting he is a failure with his public. A reviewer must be a journalist before he is a reviewer.' He was the first to make books 'news'. He had never been able to tolerate the professional *de haut en bas* of such as George Saintsbury and Churton Collins, Walter Raleigh and Ernest Dowden—though he granted that Saintsbury did occasionally 'put on the semblance of a male human being as distinguished from an asexual pedagogue.' He was often witty about writers (usually dead) for whom he did not care. Of the eighteenth-century novelist, Samuel Richardson, he observed, 'Life is far longer than it used to be, but it is still far too short for *Clarissa*'; of Charles Kingsley, 'he never uses two words if eight or ten will do'; of James, 'It took me years to ascertain that Henry James's work was giving me little pleasure.' He abhorred what he termed 'the lying that goes on about what you like and what you don't like'. He was immune from professional jealousy, unprejudiced, magnanimous, kind whenever he could conscientiously be so. In word and deed he was against the peculiarly nauseating literary *snobisme* that had already begun to alienate the public from all but the most ephemeral fiction. But he never fell into the unctuous writing of such younger contemporaries as Robert Lynd or J. C. Squire.

If one word only had to serve to describe the best of Bennett's fiction and non-fiction it would be 'honest'. It would fit the man, too.

ARNOLD BENNETT

A Select Bibliography

(Place of publication London, unless stated otherwise)

Bibliography:

ARNOLD BENNETT, 1867–1931: A Bibliography, by Norman Emery; Stoke-on-Trent (1967).

ARNOLD BENNETT: The Centenary of his birth: An Exhibition in the Berg Collection, by John D. Gordon; New York (1968)

—a select list of Bennett's books and manuscripts in the Berg Collection.

Collected Editions:

THE MINERVA EDITION, 7 vols (1926).

THE CLAYHANGER FAMILY (1925)

—contains *Clayhanger* and its two sequels, *Hilda Lessways* and *These Twain*.

THE ARNOLD BENNETT OMNIBUS BOOK (1931)

—contains *Riceyman Steps, Elsie and the Child, Lord Raingo,* and *Accident.*

THE PENGUIN ARNOLD BENNETT (1954–   ).

Letters and Journals:

THINGS THAT INTERESTED ME: Being leaves from a journal kept by Arnold Bennett (1906)

—followed in 1907 and 1908 by two further series called *Things which have interested me,* all privately printed.

JOURNAL, 1929 (1930).

THE JOURNALS OF ARNOLD BENNETT, 1896–1931, ed. N. Flower, 3 vols (1932–33)

—Vol. I: 1896–1910; Vol. II: 1911–1921; Vol. III: 1921–1928.

ARNOLD BENNETT'S LETTERS TO HIS NEPHEW [Richard Bennett] (1935).

ARNOLD BENNETT: A Portrait done at home. Together with 170 letters from A. B. to D. C. B. [Dorothy M. C. Bennett] (1935).

THE JOURNALS OF ARNOLD BENNETT, selected and edited by F. Swinnerton (1954)

— a later edition, 1971, includes newly discovered Vol. 6 of Journal (21 Sept. 1906 – 18 July 1907) and Florentine Journal.

ARNOLD BENNETT and H. G. WELLS: A Record of a personal and literary friendship, ed. H. Wilson (1960)

—mainly letters between the two men, 1897–1930.

CORRESPONDANCE ANDRÉ GIDE – ARNOLD BENNETT: Vingt ans d'amitié littéraire, 1911–1931, ed. L. F. Brugmans; Geneva (1964).

FLORENTINE JOURNAL, 1st April–25th May 1910 (1967)
—illustrated by the author. Reprinted in 2nd ed. of *The Journals of Arnold Bennett*, ed. F. Swinnerton, 1971.
LETTERS OF ARNOLD BENNETT, ed. J. Hepburn (1966–70)
—Vol. I: Letters to J. B. Pinker; Vol. II: 1889–1915; Vol. III: 1916–1931.

Separate Works:

A MAN FROM THE NORTH (1898). *Novel*
JOURNALISM FOR WOMEN: A Practical guide (1898). *Essay*
POLITE FARCES FOR THE DRAWING-ROOM (1900). *Drama*
—contains *The Stepmother, A Good Woman, A Question of Sex*, afterwards published separately in a series called Repertory Plays.
FAME AND FICTION: An Enquiry into certain popularities (1901). *Criticism*
THE GRAND BABYLON HOTEL: A Fantasia on modern themes (1902). *Novel*
—published in the United States under the title *T. Racksole and Daughter*. First of the humorous and sensational novels to which Bennett gave the description *Fantasias*. They were written to be printed in instalments as serial stories for popular journals, and were sold outright to Tillotson's Newspaper Syndicate.
ANNA OF THE FIVE TOWNS: A Novel (1902).
THE GATES OF WRATH: A Melodrama (1903). *Novel*
—one of the 'Fantasias'.
THE TRUTH ABOUT AN AUTHOR (1903). *Autobiography*
—published anonymously after serialization in *The Academy*.
HOW TO BECOME AN AUTHOR: A Practical guide (1903).
LEONORA: A Novel (1903).
A GREAT MAN: A Frolic (1904). *Novel*
TERESA OF WATLING STREET: A Fantasia on modern themes (1904). *Novel*
TALES OF THE FIVE TOWNS (1905)
—contains: 'His Worship the Goosedriver', 'The Elixir of Youth', 'Mary with the High Hand', 'The Dog', 'A Feud', 'Phantom', 'Tiddy-fol-lol', 'The Idiot', 'The Hungarian Rhapsody', 'The Sisters Quita', 'Nocturne at the Majestic', 'Clarice of the Autumn Concerts', 'A Letter Home' (Bennett's first short story, originally published in *The Yellow Book*).
THE LOOT OF CITIES: Being the adventures of a millionaire in search of joy: A Fantasia (1905). *Short Stories*
SACRED AND PROFANE LOVE: A Novel in three episodes (1905)
—published in the United States under the title *The Book of Carlotta*, 1911. Dramatized version, 1919.
HUGO: A Fantasia on modern themes (1906). *Novel*
WHOM GOD HATH JOINED (1906). *Novel*
THE SINEWS OF WAR: A Romance of London and the sea (1906). *Novel*
—in collaboration with Eden Phillpotts. Published in the United States under the title of *Doubloons*.

THE GHOST: A Fantasia on modern themes (1907). *Novel*
—the first of the 'Fantasias' to be written. Serialized in 1899 as 'For Love and Life'.
THE REASONABLE LIFE: Being hints for men and women (1907)
—revised and reprinted as *Mental Efficiency*, 1912. First of the short books of advice on self-help which the publishers called 'Arnold Bennett's Pocket Philosophies'. Composed of sets of articles, the 'Savoir Vivre Papers', etc. contributed to *T.P.'s Weekly*.
THE GRIM SMILE OF THE FIVE TOWNS (1907). *Short Stories*
—contains: 'The Lion's Share', 'Baby's Bath', 'The Silent Brothers', 'The Nineteenth Hat', 'Vera's First Christmas Adventure', 'The Murder of the Mandarin', 'Vera's Second Christmas Adventure', 'The Burglary', 'News of the Engagement', 'Beginning the New Year', 'From One Generation to Another', 'The Death of Simon Fuge', 'In a New Bottle'.
THE CITY OF PLEASURE: A Fantasia on Modern Themes (1907). *Novel*
THE STATUE (1908). *Novel*
—in collaboration with Eden Phillpotts.
HOW TO LIVE ON 24 HOURS A DAY (1908)
—a 'Pocket Philosophy'.
BURIED ALIVE: A Tale of these days (1908). *Novel*
—dramatized version, under the title *The Great Adventure*, 1912.
THE OLD WIVES' TALE: A Novel (1908).
THE HUMAN MACHINE (1908)
—a 'Pocket Philosophy'.
CUPID AND COMMONSENSE: A Play in four acts (1909).
—a dramatization of *Anna of the Five Towns*.
WHAT THE PUBLIC WANTS (1909). *Drama*
—first published as a supplement to *The English Review*.
LITERARY TASTE: How to Form it. With Instructions for Collecting a Complete Library of English Literature (1909).
THE GLIMPSE: An Adventure of the soul (1909). *Novel*
HELEN WITH THE HIGH HAND: An Idyllic diversion (1910). *Novel*
—serialized as 'The Miser's Niece'. Dramatized version by Richard Pryce, 1912.
CLAYHANGER (1910). *Novel*
—the first volume of a trilogy afterwards collected in one volume as *The Clayhanger Family* (1925).
THE CARD: A Story of Adventure in the Five Towns (1911). *Novel*
—serialized, and published in the United States, under the title *Denry the Audacious*.
HILDA LESSWAYS (1911). *Novel*
—a sequel to *Clayhanger*.
THE HONEYMOON: A Comedy in three acts (1910).
THE FEAST OF ST FRIEND (1911)
—one of the 'Pocket Philosophies'; on Christmas. Published in the United States and in later British editions under the title *Friendship and Happiness*.

THE MATADOR OF THE FIVE TOWNS, AND OTHER STORIES (1912)
—contains: 'The Matador of the Five Towns', 'Mimi', 'The Supreme Illusion', 'The Letter and the Lie', 'The Glimpse' (first draft of the novel of that name), 'Jock-at-a-Venture', 'The Heroism of Thomas Chadwick', 'Under the Clock', 'Three Episodes in the Life of Mr Cowlishaw, Dentist', 'Catching the Train', 'The Widow of the Balcony', 'The Cat and Cupid', 'The Fortune-Teller', 'The Long-lost Uncle', 'The Tight Hand', 'Why the Clock Stopped', 'Hot Potatoes', 'Half-a-Sovereign', 'The Blue Suit', 'The Tiger and the Baby', 'The Revolver', 'An Unfair Advantage'.

MILESTONES: A Play in three acts (1912).
—in collaboration with Edward Knoblauch [Knoblock]. Serialized in *Munsey's Magazine*.

THOSE UNITED STATES (1912). *Commentary*
—published in the United States under the title *Your United States*. Serialized in *Harper's Magazine*.

THE REGENT: A Five Towns story of adventure in London (1913). *Novel*
—published in the United States under the the the title *The Old Adam*.

THE PLAIN MAN AND HIS WIFE (1913)
—one of the 'Pocket Philosophies'. Published in the United States under the title *Married Life*.

PARIS NIGHTS AND OTHER IMPRESSIONS OF PLACES AND PEOPLE (1913). *Descriptive and Social Essays.*
—contains: 'Paris Nights' (1910), 'Life in London' (1911), 'Italy' (1910), 'The Riviera' (1907), 'Fontainebleau' (1904–1909), 'Switzerland' (1909–1911), 'England Again' (1907), 'The Midlands' (1910–1911), 'The British Home' (1908), 'Streets, Roads and Trains' (1907–1909). With illustrations by E. A. Rickards, FRIBA.

THE PRICE OF LOVE: A Tale (1914). *Novel*

THE AUTHOR'S CRAFT (1914). *Criticism*
—published in 1915, although dated 1914.

LIBERTY: A Statement of the British Case (1914)
—discussion of the causes of the First World War.

FROM THE LOG OF THE VELSA; New York (1914)
—contains: 'Holland', 'The Baltic', 'Copenhagen', 'On the French and Flemish Coasts', 'East Anglian Estuaries'. English edition not published until 1920. With frontispiece in colour by the Author and many illustrations by E. A. Rickards.

OVER THERE: War Scenes on the Western Front (1915).

THESE TWAIN (1916). *Novel*
—third and concluding volume of the trilogy afterwards published in 1925 as an omnibus volume called *The Clayhanger Family*.

THE LION'S SHARE (1916). *Novel*

BOOKS AND PERSONS: Being Comments on a Past Epoch, 1908–11 (1917).
—reprinted causeries first published in *The New Age* in the years indicated, under the pseudonym 'Jacob Tonson'.

THE PRETTY LADY: A Novel (1918).
THE TITLE: A Comedy in three acts (1918).
SELF AND SELF-MANAGEMENT: Essays about existing (1918).
—one of the 'Pocket Philosophies'.
THE ROLL-CALL (1918). *Novel*
JUDITH: A Play in three acts founded on the Apocryphal Book of
   Judith (1919)
—a version of this play, *Judith: An Opera in one act*, with libretto by
   Bennett and music by Eugene Goossens, was published in 1929.
OUR WOMEN: Chapters on the Sex-Discord (1920). *Essay*
THINGS THAT HAVE INTERESTED ME (1921). *Essays*
—followed by a second and third series in 1923 and 1926. These are
   distinct from the earlier series with a similar title—see *Letters and
   Journals* section above.
MR PROHACK (1922). *Novel*
—dramatized in collaboration with Edward Knoblock, 1927.
BODY AND SOUL: A Play in four acts (1922).
THE LOVE MATCH: A Play in five scenes (1922).
LILIAN (1922). *Novel*
HOW TO MAKE THE BEST OF LIFE (1923). *Essay*
—one of the 'Pocket Philosophies'.
DON JUAN DE MARANA: A Play in four acts (1923).
RICEYMAN STEPS: A Novel (1923).
LONDON LIFE: A Play (1924).
—in collaboration with Edward Knoblock.
THE BRIGHT ISLAND (1924). *Drama*
ELSIE AND THE CHILD: A Tale of Riceyman Steps and Other Stories
   (1924)
—contains 'Elsie and the Child', 'During Dinner', 'The Paper Cap',
   'The Box-office Girl', 'Mr Jack Hollins against Fate', 'Nine o'Clock
   Tomorrow', 'The Yacht', 'Outside and Inside', 'Last Love', 'The
   Mysterious Destruction of Mr Ipple', 'The Perfect Creature', 'The
   Fish', 'The Limits of Dominion'.
LORD RAINGO (1926). *Novel*
THE WOMAN WHO STOLE EVERYTHING, AND OTHER STORIES (1927)
—contains: 'The Woman Who Stole Everything', 'A Place in
   Venice', 'The Toreador', 'Middle-Aged', 'The Umbrella', 'House
   to Let', 'Claribel', 'Time to Think', 'One of Their Quarrels',
   'What I Have Said I Have Said', 'Death, Fire, and Life', 'The
   Epidemic', 'A Very Romantic Affair'.
THE STRANGE VANGUARD: A Fantasia (1928). *Novel*
—published in the United States under the title *The Vanguard*.
MEDITERRANEAN SCENES: Rome, Greece, Constantinople (1928)
—the edition, with collotype illustrations reproducing photographs
   of architecture, statuary, and paintings, was limited to 1,000 copies.
THE SAVOUR OF LIFE: Essays in gusto (1928). *Essays*
—reprinted articles, some of them discussions on new books contributed to the *Evening Standard*.

ACCIDENT (1929). *Novel*
PICCADILLY: Story of the film (1929).
THE RELIGIOUS INTERREGNUM (1929). *Essay*
—a contribution to a series of booklets called 'Affirmations'.
IMPERIAL PALACE (1930). *Novel*
THE NIGHT VISITOR, AND OTHER STORIES (1931)
—contains: 'The Night Visitor', 'The Cornet-Player', 'Murder!',
'The Hat', 'Under the Hammer', 'The Wind', 'Honour', 'The
First Night', 'The Seven Policemen', 'Myrtle at 6 a.m.', 'Strange
Affair at an Hotel', 'The Second Night', 'The Understudy', 'The
Peacock', 'Dream', 'Baccarat', 'The Mouse and the Cat'.
VENUS RISING FROM THE SEA (1931). *Short Story*
—with illustrations by E. McKnight Kauffer.
DREAM OF DESTINY: An Unfinished Novel, and, VENUS RISING FROM THE
SEA (1932). *Novel and Short Story*
'THE SNAKE CHARMER'. In: EIGHT ONE-ACT PLAYS (1933).
'FLORA'. In: FIVE THREE-ACT PLAYS (1933).
ARNOLD BENNETT: The *Evening Standard* years: Books and persons,
1926-1931, ed. Andrew Mylett (1974).
—a collection of his weekly articles in the London newspaper,
Evening Standard.

Some Critical and Biographical Studies:
ARNOLD BENNETT, by F. J. Harvey Darton (1915)
—new edition, 1924.
THE PROBLEM OF ARNOLD BENNETT, by G. West [G. H. Wells] (1923).
ARNOLD BENNETT OF THE FIVE TOWNS, by L. G. Johnson (1924).
MR BENNETT AND MRS BROWN, by Virginia Woolf (1924)
—anti-Bennett study by a younger novelist, member of the Blooms-
bury group.
ARNOLD BENNETT, by Marguerite Bennett (1925)
—by his French wife.
FOUR CONTEMPORARY NOVELISTS, by Wilbur L. Cross; New York
(1930)
—a study of Conrad, Bennett, Galsworthy and Wells.
MY ARNOLD BENNETT, by Marguerite Bennett (1931)
—not always factually accurate.
'A. B.': . . A Minor Marginal Note by Pauline Smith (1933).
ARNOLD BENNETT UND FRANKREICH, by Ruth Jaeschke; Breslau (1934).
ARNOLD BENNETT: A Portrait Done at Home, by Dorothy Cheston
Bennett (1935)
—by his second wife, the actress Dorothy Cheston.
FRAUENGESTALTEN IN ARNOLD BENNETTS ROMANEN, by E. Drabert;
Bonn (1936).
ARNOLD BENNETT AND HIS NOVELS: A Critical Study, by Jacob B.
Simons; Oxford (1936).
DIE ROMANTISCHEN ELEMENTE IN ARNOLD BENNETT, by Elisabeth
Massoulard; Bonn (1938).

ARNOLD BENNETT, by Georges Lafourcade (1939)
—still the most acute analytical study of Bennett's writings.
LA JEUNESSE D'ARNOLD BENNETT, 1867–1904, by Margaret Locherbie-Goff; Avesnes-sur-Helpe (1939).
ARNOLD BENNETT, by W. Allen (1948).
ARNOLD BENNETT, by Frank Swinnerton (1950)
—sympathetic study by a younger friend.
ARNOLD BENNETT: A Biography, by Reginald Pound (1952).
—the best and fullest life; less satisfactory on the works.
ARNOLD BENNETT E I ROMANZI DELLE CINQUE CITTÀ, by Vittoria Sanna; Florence (1953).
ARNOLD BENNETT: Primitivism and taste, by James W. Hall; Seattle (1959).
THE ART OF ARNOLD BENNETT, by James G. Hepburn; Bloomington, Indiana (1963).
WRITER BY TRADE: A View of Arnold Bennett, by Dudley Barker (1966).
THE MASTER: A Study of Arnold Bennett, by Oswald H. Davis (1966).
ARNOLD BENNETT AND STOKE-ON-TRENT, by Ernest J. D. Warrillow; Hanley, Stoke-on-Trent (1966).
ARNOLD BENNETT CENTENARY, 1867–1967; Hanley, Stoke-on-Trent (1967)
—an illustrated brochure.
ARNOLD BENNETT ET SES ROMANS RÉALISTES, by Louis Tillier; Paris (1967).
THE AUTHOR'S CRAFT AND OTHER CRITICAL WRITINGS OF ARNOLD BENNETT, ed. Samuel Hynes; Lincoln, Nebraska (1968).
STUDIES IN THE SOURCES OF ARNOLD BENNETT'S NOVELS, by Louis Tillier; Paris (1969)
—revealing, scholarly inquiry.
ARNOLD BENNETT IN LOVE: Arnold Bennett and his wife Marguerite Soulié: A correspondence, edited and translated by George & Jean Beardmore (1972).
ARNOLD BENNETT: A Biography, by Margaret Drabble (1974)
—enthusiastic, well-informed appreciation by a young novelist unborn when Bennett died.

WRITERS AND THEIR WORK

GRAY: R. W. Ketton-Cremer
HUME: Montgomery Belgion
SAMUEL JOHNSON: S. C. Roberts
POPE: Ian Jack
RICHARDSON: R. F. Brissenden
SHERIDAN: W. A. Darlington
CHRISTOPHER SMART: G. Grigson
SMOLLETT: Laurence Brander
STEELE, ADDISON: A. R. Humphreys
STERNE: D. W. Jefferson
SWIFT: J. Middleton Murry
SIR JOHN VANBRUGH: Bernard Harris
HORACE WALPOLE: Hugh Honour

Nineteenth Century:
MATTHEW ARNOLD: Kenneth Allott
JANE AUSTEN: S. Townsend Warner
BAGEHOT: N. St John-Stevas
THE BRONTËS: I & II: Winifred Gérin
BROWNING: John Bryson
E. B. BROWNING: Alethea Hayter
SAMUEL BUTLER: G. D. H. Cole
BYRON: I, II & III: Bernard Blackstone
CARLYLE: David Gascoyne
LEWIS CARROLL: Derek Hudson
COLERIDGE: Kathleen Raine
CREEVEY & GREVILLE: J. Richardson
DE QUINCEY: Hugh Sykes Davies
DICKENS: K. J. Fielding
    EARLY NOVELS: T. Blount
    LATER NOVELS: B. Hardy
DISRAELI: Paul Bloomfield
GEORGE ELIOT: Lettice Cooper
FERRIER & GALT: W. M. Parker
FITZGERALD: Joanna Richardson
ELIZABETH GASKELL: Miriam Allott
GISSING: A. C. Ward
THOMAS HARDY: R. A. Scott-James
                    and C. Day Lewis
HAZLITT: J. B. Priestley
HOOD: Laurence Brander
G. M. HOPKINS: Geoffrey Grigson
T. H. HUXLEY: William Irvine
KEATS: Edmund Blunden
LAMB: Edmund Blunden
LANDOR: G. Rostrevor Hamilton
EDWARD LEAR: Joanna Richardson
MACAULAY: G. R. Potter

MEREDITH: Phyllis Bartlett
JOHN STUART MILL: M. Cranston
WILLIAM MORRIS: P. Henderson
NEWMAN: J. M. Cameron
PATER: Ian Fletcher
PEACOCK: J. I. M. Stewart
ROSSETTI: Oswald Doughty
CHRISTINA ROSSETTI: G. Battiscombe
RUSKIN: Peter Quennell
SIR WALTER SCOTT: Ian Jack
SHELLEY: G. M. Matthews
SOUTHEY: Geoffrey Carnall
LESLIE STEPHEN: Phyllis Grosskurth
R. L. STEVENSON: G. B. Stern
SWINBURNE: Ian Fletcher
TENNYSON: B. C. Southam
THACKERAY: Laurence Brander
FRANCIS THOMPSON: P. Butter
TROLLOPE: Hugh Sykes Davies
OSCAR WILDE: James Laver
WORDSWORTH: Helen Darbishire

Twentieth Century:
CHINUA ACHEBE: A. Ravenscroft
JOHN ARDEN: Glenda Leeming
W. H. AUDEN: Richard Hoggart
SAMUEL BECKETT: J-J. Mayoux
HILAIRE BELLOC: Renée Haynes
ARNOLD BENNETT: Kenneth Young
EDMUND BLUNDEN: Alec M. Hardie
ROBERT BRIDGES: J. Sparrow
ANTHONY BURGESS: Carol M. Dix
ROY CAMPBELL: David Wright
JOYCE CARY: Walter Allen
G. K. CHESTERTON: C. Hollis
WINSTON CHURCHILL: John Connell
R. G. COLLINGWOOD: E. W. F. Tomlin
I. COMPTON-BURNETT:
                    R. Glynn Grylls
JOSEPH CONRAD: Oliver Warner
WALTER DE LA MARE: K. Hopkins
NORMAN DOUGLAS: Ian Greenlees
LAWRENCE DURRELL: G. S. Fraser
T. S. ELIOT: M. C. Bradbrook
T. S. ELIOT: The Making of
    'The Waste Land': M. C. Bradbrook
FORD MADOX FORD: Kenneth Young
E. M. FORSTER: Rex Warner

CHRISTOPHER FRY: Derek Stanford
JOHN GALSWORTHY: R. H. Mottram
WILLIAM GOLDING: Stephen Medcalf
ROBERT GRAVES: M. Seymour-Smith
GRAHAM GREENE: Francis Wyndham
L. P. HARTLEY: Paul Bloomfield
A. E. HOUSMAN: Ian Scott-Kilvert
TED HUGHES: Keith Sagar
ALDOUS HUXLEY: Jocelyn Brooke
HENRY JAMES: Michael Swan
PAMELA HANSFORD JOHNSON:
                                    Isabel Quigly
JAMES JOYCE: J. I. M. Stewart
RUDYARD KIPLING: Bonamy Dobrée
D. H. LAWRENCE: Kenneth Young
DORIS LESSING: Michael Thorpe
C. DAY LEWIS: Clifford Dyment
WYNDHAM LEWIS: E. W. F. Tomlin
COMPTON MACKENZIE: K. Young
LOUIS MACNEICE: John Press
KATHERINE MANSFIELD: Ian Gordon
JOHN MASEFIELD: L. A. G. Strong
SOMERSET MAUGHAM: J. Brophy
GEORGE MOORE: A. Norman Jeffares
J. MIDDLETON MURRY:
                                    Philip Mairet
R. K. NARAYAN: William Walsh
SEAN O'CASEY: W. A. Armstrong
GEORGE ORWELL: Tom Hopkinson

JOHN OSBORNE: Simon Trussler
HAROLD PINTER: John Russell Taylor
POETS OF 1939–45 WAR:
                                    R. N. Currey
ANTHONY POWELL:
                                    Bernard Bergonzi
POWYS BROTHERS: R. C. Churchill
J. B. PRIESTLEY: Ivor Brown
PROSE WRITERS OF WORLD WAR I:
                                    M. S. Greicus
HERBERT READ: Francis Berry
PETER SHAFFER: John Russell Taylor
BERNARD SHAW: A. C. Ward
EDITH SITWELL: John Lehmann
KENNETH SLESSOR: C. Semmler
C. P. SNOW: William Cooper
MURIEL SPARK: Patricia Stubbs
DAVID STOREY: John Russell Taylor
SYNGE & LADY GREGORY: E. Coxhead
DYLAN THOMAS: G. S. Fraser
G. M. TREVELYAN: J. H. Plumb
WAR POETS: 1914–18: E. Blunden
EVELYN WAUGH: Christopher Hollis
H. G. WELLS: Kenneth Young
ARNOLD WESKER: Glenda Leeming
PATRICK WHITE: R. F. Brissenden
ANGUS WILSON: K. W. Gransden
VIRGINIA WOOLF: B. Blackstone
W. B. YEATS: G. S. Fraser